"Barry Rowan has written a book about a th[...] *Business* can transform the way you think abou[...] your work. Based on his own remarkable career, Barry's book takes you into the unvarnished crucible of the workplace—with all its gritty challenges, victories, setbacks, and difficult people—and shows you how your career can become a sacred and purposeful journey instead of just a daily and exhausting grind. Spend a few hours with Barry, and he will show you how God intends to repurpose you. *The Spiritual Art of Business* is a book that can transform the next few decades of your career."

Richard Stearns, president emeritus of World Vision US and author of *Lead Like It Matters to God*

"Working through *The Spiritual Art of Business* is a thought-provoking, spiritually enriching endeavor that can transform our relationship with God and our work. Barry Rowan's short and practical chapters reflect his own deep wrestling with God about the meaning of his work and all the accompanying trials and rewards. He launches us into our own 'archaeological dig' into the feelings, beliefs, and habits that so often encumber our experience of work. Do a chapter each day, using the probing reflection questions at the end, and allow yourself to be drawn deeper into the freedom and adventure available through a life of following Christ."

Katherine Leary Alsdorf, founding director of Redeemer City to City's Center for Faith and Work, and consultant for faith and work ministry development

"In a conversational style that feels like a fireside chat with an old friend, Barry Rowan has distilled his study of the Bible and decades of experience as a senior executive in *The Spiritual Art of Business*. Each chapter is a nugget of wisdom, and the reader will be rewarded for remembering the stories and taking seriously the questions that Barry poses."

Scott Stephenson, former chairman and chief executive officer of Verisk Analytics

"In *The Spiritual Art of Business*, Barry Rowan takes us on a forty-day journey of submission and renewal in Christ. A seasoned C-suite executive, Rowan has thought deeply about the theological and practical realities of God working through him in the marketplace. And in this study he takes us on a four-part journey of surrender, transformation, realignment, and fulfillment. It's a journey every Christ-follower in business should take, and Barry is a worthy guide and mentor in this important spiritual work."

John Coleman, managing partner of Sovereign's Capital and author of *The HBR Guide to Crafting Your Purpose*

"Barry Rowan's decades spent in senior leadership experience are set in a new light in *The Spiritual Art of Business* as he humbly calls Christians to a life of surrender and service. In laying down our personal desires and plans, we can pursue transformed lives, ones realigned with God's purpose."

D. Michael Lindsay, president of Taylor University and author of *Hinge Moments*

"God has a purpose for us, explains the apostle Paul in Romans 8:28. In *The Spiritual Art of Business*, Barry Rowan uses his life as a perfect example of God purposefully using his work. The wonderful reflection questions at the end of every chapter allow readers to deeply examine their lives, especially relating to their work. I recommend this book to anyone in the workplace. It would especially be great for a small group or book club to go through together, then touch base periodically afterward. God does have a purpose for all of us in our work, in different ways and at different times, to be his light on earth."

Diane Paddison, founder and president of 4word and author of *Work, Love, Pray*

"This is a truly helpful work, integrating deep spiritual lessons with the call to serve God and others in the business arena. The short chapters that conclude with penetrating reflection questions are perfect for creating space to do your own integrative work. It is both a blessing and a challenge!"

Ruth Haley Barton, founder of the Transforming Center and author of *Strengthening the Soul of Your Leadership*

"I have long admired how Barry Rowan integrates his commitment to God with his daily business practices. This book is a wise distillation of his learning, hard won over a wide-ranging career marked by both successes and failures. Through short and accessible chapters, Rowan encourages us to surrender our work to God, allow God to use our work to transform us, realign our work with God's purposes, and contribute to a better world through our work. This is a book to be read slowly, savored, and revisited over time."

Denise Daniels, Hudson T. Harrison Professor of Entrepreneurship at Wheaton College and author of *Working in the Presence of God*

THE
SPIRITUAL
ART
OF
BUSINESS

CONNECTING THE DAILY
WITH THE DIVINE

BARRY L. ROWAN

An imprint of InterVarsity Press
Downers Grove, Illinois

InterVarsity Press
P.O. Box 1400 | Downers Grove, IL 60515-1426
ivpress.com | email@ivpress.com

InterVarsity Press® is the publishing division of InterVarsity Christian Fellowship/US®. For more information, visit intervarsity.org.

Cover design: David Fassett
Interior design: Jeanna Wiggins

ISBN 978-1-5140-0762-4 (print) | ISBN 978-1-5140-0763-1 (digital)

Printed in the United States of America ∞

| **Library of Congress Cataloging-in-Publication Data** |
| A catalog record for this book is available from the Library of Congress. |

29 28 27 26 25 24 23 | 13 12 11 10 9 8 7 6 5 4 3 2 1

**TO MY WIFE, LINDA,
AND OUR SONS,
MARK AND DAVID,**

for journeying with me through the decades to make our lives and our work meaningful. Thank you for your patience and your love.

CONTENTS

PREFACE

● ● ●

When I was a few weeks shy of my twenty-ninth birthday, fissures deep within me were exposed in a dramatic eruption.

I'd climbed up to a red rock outcropping above a camp in Colorado and was sitting alone, absorbing the warmth of the afternoon sun. It was late summer and the landscape stretched out before me, a thousand feet down the shoulder of the mountain, across the Arkansas River Valley, and on to the glowing foothills and expansive plains beyond.

The world was at peace.

I was not.

Perhaps it was the harmony of nature exposing the disharmony within me, but without warning or explanation, I exploded in tears. Within moments the tears inexplicably accelerated into convulsive sobs of raw emotion. My soul was in anguish, and my body was shaking. *Where is this emotion coming from? And why now?*

I had good reasons for asking myself those questions. I was young. I was healthy. I was blessed with a joyous, life-giving marriage, and an abundance of friends. My career was off to a strong start. So what was stirring this cauldron of emotion?

Even then, I knew the ache of the outburst was not born in that instant. A steely will and a deep longing for God had lived under a fragile treaty within me since my earliest years. And a shadowy confusion had been my companion since my college days as I wrestled with what major and career to pursue. Over time, the confusion had only deepened. In the agony on that rock, the questions were now screaming at me: *Why am I alive? Will I live a successful life? What is a successful life? Why am I working so hard? By what measure will I judge the success of my life?*

The divide within me was laid bare that day in the Colorado mountains—a crisis over meaning in work had come to a head.

After that day, I could no longer ignore the questions burning within me. Over the next eight years, I read dozens of books and attended multiple workshops. I spent untold hours in the Scriptures, prayed and talked with people, wrote hundreds of pages in my journal, and listened and looked for God through the fog—all with the hope of understanding how to approach my work in a way that matters.

For starters, I realized this was actually about something much bigger than *meaning in work*. It was about *purpose in life*. The God who I was no longer sure existed had to provide clarity about purpose in life as a context for understanding meaning in work. He had to strip away my beliefs built over thirty years of sitting in the pews, taking me down to the bedrock of my being. Through the anguish, fundamental questions emerged like, *Does God exist?* And if he does, *Am I willing to live my life for him instead of myself?* After six months of reading and pondering, and many middle-of-the-night scribblings in my journal, I was able to take the key step toward addressing the question of purpose in life. I chose to believe in God based, as the lawyers would say, on the preponderance of the evidence and would give up everything I have to follow Jesus.

In the end, what I learned about the question of meaning in work was that I'd had it backward: We don't derive meaning *from* our work; we bring meaning *to* our work. And God's perspective of our work is the source of its ultimate meaning.

There is no true meaning in our lives or in our work apart from God. As I have surrendered my life to him, he has lovingly led me, and is making me into the shape that seems best to him. As the clay of my soul has softened and become more supple in his hands, God is able to use me more effectively for his purposes, including the work I've been given to do.

I began to see that my work was no longer in one part of my life and my faith in another. The divide had been bridged. As a person called to business, I experience God's work within my work. It's an ongoing metamorphosis that begins not in me, but in God, and radiates outward from him through me and into the world.

This new perspective on work has animated my work life for the last thirty years. I've spent my career in senior leadership positions, building or turning around eight businesses, including serving as the CEO, president, and division manager for three of them, as well as CFO for four public companies. Six of the businesses have been successful, with one selling for $10 billion, and two were not. God has been there with me throughout the highs and the lows, teaching me, growing me, and asking me to serve as an instrument of his will.

As the people who have known me for decades can attest, I'm a different person than I was in the early years of my career: Peaceful when I used to easily become fearful. Still setting high standards, but no longer driven to prove myself. Seeing my work as an expression of who I am rather than letting it define who I am. Freer and less constrained. And increasingly filled with a sustaining joy. I am deeply grateful for these changes that have been wrought in me, knowing it is the work of God, and he who has begun a good work in us will bring it to completion.

HOW THIS BOOK CAN HELP YOU

Most of us who are reflective about our work sooner or later face a common problem: We live in fear of living a meaningless life. We want the hundred thousand hours we will work in our lifetime to matter. We want to live a life of significance. This was behind the outburst on the rock that day, and this fear haunted me during the earlier years of my career. It's probably one you're wrestling with too. I can tell you out of my own experience that this issue will eat us alive over time if we don't commit to resolving it.

The good news is that God has a perspective of our work, and if we live within the divine design, we will live a life of deep, profound meaning. If we allow him to, God *will* transform us, so that he might transform the world through us. Is there any greater joy than being used by the Creator of the universe as an instrument of his will?

While these writings represent a life of integrated contemplation and action, they are not directed toward monks in the desert or one planning to spend her life in the cloister (though those can be perfectly legitimate callings). These readings and reflections are designed for those who seek meaning and peace even as they are called to live and work in the harshness of this world.

This can include people in any kind of work or any form of leadership—members of the C-suite, mid-level managers, and manual laborers; entrepreneurs, small-business owners, and creative gig workers; teachers, stay-at-home parents, ministry leaders; and more. This time we will spend together is meant for anyone interested in developing a life-giving perspective of their work as seen through the eyes of God.

The only qualification is that you are open-minded and willing to submit to the love and lessons of God. He may show you places within yourself that you hadn't seen before and point you to places you never considered going. If that happens, I encourage you not to hesitate to go where he leads. The journey with God is the greatest adventure this life has to offer.

As you engage with *The Spiritual Art of Business*, you will observe a cumulative arc to our conversation. It goes like this:

1. We begin by surrendering our all to Jesus.
2. Our lives are transformed as we go from living for ourselves to living according to God's dynamic design.
3. We are realigned with God's purposes, and we then live, work, and relate differently as new creations.
4. God then sends us into the world and transforms the world through us.

Figure 1. The Spiritual Art of Business cycle

Note that the Spiritual Art of Business cycle starts in the world and ends in the world. As we surrender our lives to Jesus, we will become increasingly detached from the world and then transformed by God so we can engage in the world for God rather than for our selfish gratification. We will increasingly understand our work not as a distraction from our faith but as an expression of it. Seen through this lens of faith, we can engage in our work with a sense of freedom, exuberance, and energy as we more fully connect the daily with the divine.

HOW TO ENTER THIS EXPERIENCE

This is a different kind of a book from most others you've read—it is intended not so much to be *read* as to be *experienced*. It is designed to be a gateway to prayer, a chance for you to stop, to be with God. It is an invitation into a conversation with God about things that matter. I encourage you to read it slowly, to absorb it, reflecting on how these ideas apply to you. It is not meant as a task to be completed but as a meal to be enjoyed.

I also encourage you to adopt a posture of openness as you enter this experience, leaning forward in anticipation of what God will do for you and in you. Expect an experience of listening more than speaking, of immersing more than analyzing.

In this context, you may choose to proceed through the chapters sequentially and at your own pace as you would any other book to experience the cumulative progression of the chapters. You may also wish to take one chapter per day, savoring the ideas in that chapter and contemplating your responses to the reflection questions throughout the day. Or, after reading the table of contents, you may choose to prioritize the readings, beginning with those that most seem to fit who you are and where you are in your journey with our dear Lord.

Each reading includes stories and insights derived from my own pursuit of meaning in work and in life. Many of them are taken from places where I've had it wrong, often for a long time. I have tried to record what has been most helpful to me, with the hope that it will also be helpful to you.

More important than sharing my own story is that each of the readings is led by a much better guide than I—the Word of God. I encourage you to read the Scripture verses slowly, perhaps using your Bible to look them up so you can see them in their broader contexts. As you enter God's Word, let the Word enter you. A central goal of this life is to have the Word become flesh in us. As has often been said, it doesn't matter how much we go through the Bible—what matters is how much of the Bible goes through us.

Each chapter ends with some questions, asking you to reflect on the state of your heart and ponder God's desires for you. Please don't shortchange this part of the experience. Each of the reflection sections is an invitation for God to meet you where you are—to listen to him, to engage with him, to share yourself with him, and to let him share himself and his love with you. This is the place where transformation truly happens.

Here's a simple tip to help solidify the new perspectives I hope you gain from this experience: write it down.

For me, writing in a journal is a continuation of my daily prayer. I find this practice to be a wonderful way to clarify and consolidate what I have learned through a time of listening to God. So even if you're not ordinarily a journaler, I encourage you to write down the things that come to mind using a notebook or a notes app. You may also find it helpful to engage with these ideas in a small group, and you can find a free discussion guide at www.barrylrowan.com.

The central idea is this: *God uses our work to do his work in us. And as we are transformed by him, he will transform the world through us.* I believe God will show you in a personalized way what this looks like for you. It's going to be a grand and beautiful vision and a journey that will last a lifetime.

PART 1

SURRENDERED

DISCOVERING FREEDOM
IN SUBMISSION TO JESUS

*As we surrender ourselves to God, we come into our
most complete selves as the Spirit of Jesus occupies
us and is expressed through us. We grow into better
employees, better bosses, and better coworkers.*

1

COME, FOLLOW ME

Those of you who do not give up everything
you have cannot be my disciples.

LUKE 14:33

> *Our natural inclination is to take control to*
> *achieve independence, but surrender is the*
> *first step on the path to true freedom.*

Jesus' first words to his disciple Peter were "Come, follow me" (Mark 1:17). They were also his last: "You must follow me" (John 21:22).

Our adventure with God begins with the decision to follow Jesus rather than our own desires. Surrender can be terrifying as we are asked to put everything on the table—our possessions, our careers, our pride, our freedom, indeed our very lives. Our natural instinct is to determine the course and lead the way. This challenge is compounded for us when we have leadership gifts we are used to exercising at work or in other aspects of our lives. In the matter of ultimate authority for our lives, however, we have to learn to follow. The best leaders are practiced followers.

In my experience, the station called Surrender is the only valid departure point for the journey toward a life of true meaning found in God. As we exchange our own plans for the plans of our Lord, it opens our eyes to see and pursue his call for our lives.

Relinquishment has become the mantra of the spiritual life for me. Surrender has revealed itself not only as the only way to step onto the Way, but also the only way to *stay* on the Way. It is the starting point . . . and the ending point.

Jesus, of course, is our greatest example of surrender. When he invites us to "Come, follow me," he is not asking us to do anything he didn't do. He did nothing apart from the Father. He came to earth with no agenda of his own—not to do his own will but to do the will of the one who sent him. His words were not his own, but rather they were the words the Father gave him. And in the end, he was obedient to the point of death—even death on a cross.

Jesus knew what was coming for him when he chose to obey the Father's will, and he tells us to count the cost of following him. And what is that cost? Only everything we have.

- "Those of you who do not give up everything you have cannot be my disciples" (Luke 14:33).
- "Whoever wants to save their life will lose it, but whoever loses their life for me will find it" (Matthew 16:25).
- "Unless a kernel of wheat falls to the ground and dies, it remains only a single seed. But if it dies, it produces many seeds" (John 12:24).

As we surrender to him, God transforms us from living a managed life to living a released life. Through our surrender, we give our gracious God permission to do his transforming work in us. He exposes the lies about our identity that we have lived by, replacing them with the truth that we are adopted sons and daughters of the Most High God. He sets us free to live into his design: life by the Spirit.

The process of reshaping, even as we wince under the pressure of the strong thumbs of the Potter, can become a source of great joy. As we live in joy, others will see the authenticity that comes from living a life where we seek, and fail, and seek again to live into the fullness of the life he has promised.

In the preface I tell the story of how a sudden outburst of tears, while I was sitting on a rock in Colorado, forced me to face questions of the meaning of my life and work. In the days that followed, I had to submit to the confusion, embrace the pain, and follow the questions. As someone who had gone to church since childhood, now at nearly thirty I had to decide whether I really believed Jesus is who he said he is. If I believed, I couldn't escape his words "Any of you who does not give up everything he has cannot be my disciple." Give up *everything*? Everything hung on the answer!

I wrestled with this admonition for weeks. The resolution came one day while I was on a run around the lake near our home. I surrendered to Jesus. I simply said to him, "I give up." (But there were certainly heel marks in the sand.)

That was thirty-five years ago. Now, as I approach the conclusion of an executive career, I sense God leading me into an "encore calling" of prayer, writing, teaching, and holistic accompaniment. I believe this season includes investing in Christ-following leaders who are called to live fully for God in the world. But . . . I can't really see how any of this is going to turn out. I have no idea whether it will be helpful to others or fulfilling to me. I have to simply put one foot in front of the other.

So the call to surrender is still very much alive within me. It's at a deeper level now, but it's also grounded in a deeper trust.

Surrender is a lifelong process that continues its work until it has worked its way into every moment, every decision, and every action we undertake. For those who wish to practice the spiritual art of business, surrender is the ground of everything.

FOR REFLECTION

- Have you declared your unconditional surrender to Jesus? Which parts of yourself, your life, or your career might you be holding back? Do you know him well enough, and trust him enough, to give up everything you have?

- Are there parts of the idea of surrender that you still find scary? What do you worry about being called to give up as part of surrender?

2

GATEWAY TO FREEDOM

Not my will, but yours be done.

LUKE 22:42

> *Abundance of life begins*
> *with abandonment to God.*

When I was in business school, a class called Control was a part of the required curriculum. I can assure you that the school didn't offer one called Surrender. The idea of surrender runs directly counter to our human instincts. What military manual would suggest surrendering to win the hill? Name a business guru who gives a keynote speech on capitulation. However, arriving at the emptiness of other alternatives through painful experience, and guided by Scripture and the Spirit, I'm learning that we must pass through the gateway of surrender to experience true freedom.

A friend of mine used to say, "If it doesn't work for you, don't export it." This wisdom has contributed to my reluctance to share truths I've read but haven't yet lived. Now, though, after decades of following Jesus, I can say that my cup is overflowing with gratitude for the fullness of life Jesus provides as we surrender to him. It flows from surrender to God wholly and in every moment of our lives. Jean Pierre de Caussade, a French Jesuit priest born in the late 1600s, called it "abandonment to divine providence."

The vantage point of surrender provides the best opportunity to see God's will and his Word embedded in every moment of our lives. And as we submit to the lessons and presence of God in each moment, we give him permission to shape us into vessels that are carriers of God himself.

To be clear, surrender is not passivity. Christ's anguish in the Garden of Gethsemane is profound evidence that it often takes more strength to let go than to hang on. It's not easy for any of us to say, "Not my will, but yours be done," over and over. We need to learn to "endure hardship as discipline" (Hebrews 12:7), because learning this lesson is the only way our lives will be nudged into alignment with God's loving design for his kingdom.

My personal transformation has included God setting me free from a perfectionism that filled a reservoir with slow-burning resentment from living in a world that is not as it should be. He is redeeming this distortion into a healthier focus on continuous improvement of myself and the world. The true God has also had to remove the false god of achievement from the gilded throne I had built for it from my earliest years as a child.

This transformation has taken years, and God and I are still working on it—and probably will be for as long as I live on this earth. We'll be touching on this process more in the chapters to come. But here in the early part of our conversation, I can state that it has all been worth it—much more than worth it.

My experience has taught me that if we submit ourselves to God's will hidden in our daily circumstances, he will also set us free from tendencies that are not necessarily selfish but that limit our humanity and our leadership.

Early in my career we hired an employee who was highly competent technically but difficult to work with personally. This manager's demeanor was combative and inflexible, introducing tension into every meeting they attended. From our individual discussions,

I knew this outward rigidity was an expression of an interior wound-edness, so I wanted to extend an extra measure of grace to this person I was responsible for hiring. We worked together over an extended period of time to improve the employee's relational skills on the job. Ultimately, though, I concluded that the disruption to the team was just too much, and we had the difficult conversation that ushered this manager out the door.

After the firing, virtually every person who had worked with this employee approached me individually to say what a relief it was to have this ill-fitting manager gone. Only then did I fully appreciate the contortions the members of our team had been going through in an effort to work with this one individual. I should have acted more quickly.

This experience dramatically and permanently expanded my understanding of compassion within the workplace. By narrowly focusing my compassion on the individual, I was being uncompassionate to the organization as a whole. The cumulative stress and stifled productivity of the team far outweighed any help I might have been to their difficult coworker. Only through surrendering my own limited notions of compassion would I gain the greater understanding I believe God was trying to teach me.

It was humbling. And freeing.

Those around us, and the voices from within, may call out, "Control! Take charge of your life. Don't lose your grip on your destiny. Protect yourself. Maintain your image." May we close our ears to these lies.

Abundance of life begins with abandonment to God.

FOR REFLECTION

- Are there times in your life when you have abandoned yourself to God's providence and experienced his abundance? What lessons did you learn from those experiences?

■ As you look at your life from your current vantage point,
   are there areas of your life where you sense God calling
   you to surrender to him so that you might receive more of
   his abundance?

■ What parts of God's abundance do you particularly long for?

3

THE TWO ROOTS OF THE RADICAL LIFE

Blessed are the poor in spirit,
for theirs is the kingdom of heaven.

MATTHEW 5:3

This is the only work God wants from you:
Believe in the one he has sent.

JOHN 6:29 NLT

> *Our surrender to God grows from*
> *the twin roots of humility and belief.*
> *Through these roots we will draw our*
> *deepest nourishment.*

The word *radical* comes from the same root as the word *radish* and literally means "root." It's truly a root word! But apart from the painful pun, it has something to teach us.

So often, when we think of something radical, it conjures up images of something "way out there." In spiritual matters, *radical* is more often rootlike, something "deep in here." The most radical way of living is in complete submission to God.

But where does this posture come from? It grows out of the twin virtues of humility and belief. I think of these as the two roots from which we draw sustenance to live the life of surrender.

Humility. "Blessed are the poor in spirit," Jesus said, "for theirs is the kingdom of heaven" (Matthew 5:3). Jesus himself took on radical poverty, and he calls us to do the same—not because he wants less for us, but because he wants more.

Humility is foundational for those of us driven to accomplish big things. Augustine said, "Do you wish to be great? Then begin by being. Do you desire to construct [something] vast and lofty? Think first about the foundations of humility. The higher your structure is to be, the deeper must be its foundations."

It takes humility to choose to follow God's will instead of our own desires in the first place, and it takes an ever-deepening humility to progress toward godliness.

- Do I have the humility to accept God's will for my life over my own will?
- Do I have the humility to embrace pain, knowing God provides purpose to our pain? To endure hardship as discipline?
- Do I have the humility to accept responsibility for my team's results when they fall short of expectations?
- Do I have the humility to admit when I'm wrong—to my superiors *and* to my subordinates?

Belief. When the disciples asked Jesus, "We want to perform God's works, too. What should we do?" the Lord simplified, and deepened, the answer by saying, "This is the only work God wants from you: Believe in the one he has sent" (John 6:28-29 NLT). Their broad question was plural ("works"). His distilled answer was singular ("believe").

We can read these words of Christ at least two ways. Our work is to believe, but it is also God's work in us. He plants belief in us so that we might live the radically abandoned life he calls us into.

But do I really believe?

- Do I believe that as I follow Jesus, my life, including my career, will not be wasted?
- Do I believe that in all things God works for the good of those who love him? In *all* things? Even the distasteful things?
- Do I believe that God will not squander the gifts he has given me? Do I believe that he is in a better position to decide the use of these gifts than I am?
- Do I believe that if I surrender this moment and my entire future to God, he will unfold the pattern of my life as he sees fit? That I will live a life of significance? That I will achieve my full potential?
- Do I believe that I will be transformed into Christ's likeness through the unceasing action of God's waves on the shores of my soul? Do I have the patience to live life in this way, waiting on the Lord to do his work?

May we aspire to be as honest in answering these questions as the father who hoped Jesus could heal his son who was unable to speak since childhood. Jesus made the incredible claim "Everything is possible for one who believes." Then the father exclaimed, "I do believe; help me overcome my unbelief!" (Mark 9:23-24).

FOR REFLECTION

- Reread the bulleted questions included above.
- Are there certain of these questions to which you can easily and honestly answer yes? Are there others where you need help in coming into a deeper humility or overcoming your unbelief?
- Can you talk with Jesus about these things honestly, as the desperate father did?

4
OUR ESSENCE
IS OUR EMPTINESS

Have the same mindset as Christ Jesus:

Who, being in very nature God,

*did not consider equality with God something
to be used to his own advantage;*

rather, he made himself nothing

by taking the very nature of a servant,

being made in human likeness.

PHILIPPIANS 2:5-7

I no longer live, but Christ lives in me.

GALATIANS 2:20

> *God empties us of ourselves
> and fills us with himself.*

As we give ourselves to God, he refines our essence into a few nuggets of pure gold and then forges this gold into a beautifully decorated chalice. We are the chalice, not the contents of the chalice. We are designed to be emptied of ourselves so we can be filled by him and with him.

Though Jesus emptied himself "by taking the very nature of a servant, being made in human likeness," I've found that I cannot empty myself. God has had to empty me of myself. He removes the contents of self from this chalice to make room for himself. In my better moments, I hope to say with Paul that it is no longer I who live but Christ who lives in me.

I've tried to fill the insatiable hunger within me with every artificial substitute, but what I've discovered is that God alone can fill us with meaning, purpose, and the things that matter—and ultimately with himself. The end state of our faith is union with God, as Jesus and the Father who is in him come and make their home with us (see John 14:23). Indeed, his home is within us. As God, who is love, fills us, the very substance of our being will be transformed from selfishness into the self-emptying love of God.

I had read of union with God for many years, but it is one thing to hear the words and another to experience the reality. I am deeply grateful to have absorbed God's overwhelming love on occasion. Sometimes he presents himself during a time of particularly deep prayer. At other times, I find myself joined with God as I am accosted with his beauty—involuntarily gasping as my eyes catch the early morning light glistening off the lake framed by the snow-covered mountains across Puget Sound. How clearly I remember feeling an inexplicable solidarity with Jesus in the people of the most impoverished areas in Central America, as they built a village for their families in the hope of a better life. The Spirit of Jesus in me connected with the Spirit of Jesus in them.

This unity has led me into an inexpressible joy as my will is forged into God's will. During these times, there is only one will. My steely will has often fought with God. But I've learned it's much better to fight the battles of life with God on our side than to fight against God from the other side. I have experienced both.

Union with God is not an abstract concept. It is a lived reality.

In my twenties, I would go into the boardroom anxious to make a good impression. Christ growing in me means that today I focus less on myself and more on advancing the purpose of the meeting. Earlier in my career, I was afraid of giving feedback to an underperforming employee, but Christ in me recognizes that the negative patterns holding them back at work are probably constricting them from experiencing the fullness of life outside of work. By speaking the truth in love, perhaps I can help them lead a more fulfilling life both at work and at home.

Later in my career, I took the CFO job with a start-up called Cool Planet Energy Systems. I joined this company because I was excited about its mission to contribute to sustainability through renewable fuels. The company was developing a technology that would produce high-octane gasoline out of wood chips. A co-product, the result of burning the wood chips, was a charcoal-like product that was good for agriculture, enabling soil to hold water and require less fertilizer.

We were nearly ready to make a go of it when oil prices dropped from $100 to $27 a barrel, decimating our business model. When we were not able to fully raise the next round of financing, we pivoted to focus on the agriculture business, which would ultimately prove to be too costly to commercialize.

I felt tremendous personal pain at seeing this business not achieve its potential either financially or in societal terms. It was like I was experiencing a death. I was D-E-A-D—to my Dreams, Expectations, Ambitions, and Desires.

I'm still processing this situation, pondering what God might be teaching me through it. I think he is showing me that even the best things of this world cannot satisfy our deepest longings, for that space can only be filled by him. As we operate in this world, there are also many things beyond our control, and we simply have to recognize our limitations.

The Cool Planet failure led me into a humility to accept that which I could not change and a belief that God's presence was there even during those difficult times. I was being emptied and filled.

How are we changed so that there is less of us and more of God? The process is more circuitous than sequential. God starts by asking us to surrender our whole life to him, and then he begins removing our impure selves from the chalice of our being. He fills this vacuum with himself and expands the size of the vessel to increase its capacity for him, so that he who is love might be poured out on the world through us.

May we cherish the moments when God pierces the veil and brings us into union with his will, showing us how his desires may become the desires of our hearts. These are the times when we are emptied of ourselves, our fingers are pried from the ersatz desires of this world, and we are filled with God alone. In these moments there is only one will, one desire. These are the most joyful times. We feel whole, needing nothing else, content with God alone, joyful in the unity we know to be him. And gratefully, these experiences are often followed by a long tail of residual light, like a comet traveling through the darkness of space.

God alone can light the deepest space within us, for it was created by him and for him.

FOR REFLECTION

- Reflect on the ways you may have been attached to the things of the world throughout your life and your career. Can you see any worldly dreams, expectations, ambitions, or desires that God may want to empty you of at this stage of your life? How might God want to detach you from these and attach you more completely to himself?

- As you reflect on your own journey with Jesus, consider some things God has had to remove from you. Perhaps these include fears or anxieties, or the desires of the old self for things such as money, prestige, or the accolades of this world. Perhaps they are things that are seemingly good, like the desire for meaningful relationships or even a life partner.

- Ask God if there are any desires he wants you to set aside so that he can expand your desire for him.

5

CRUCIBLE OF THE SOUL

You, God, tested us;
you refined us like silver.

PSALM 66:10

> **God uses our work to do his work in us.**

I like business. I derive great satisfaction from developing a clear strategy out of the spaghetti of confusing alternatives. I love setting aggressive goals and achieving them with people I enjoy and respect. I'm grateful when we meet the challenge of raising capital for a rapidly growing company, as mandated by the bronze plaque engraved for me by my coworkers where I had my first CFO job: "DROOC—Don't Run Out Of Cash." I enjoy sitting across the table from a customer, listening to them describe their needs and marshaling the resources of our company to fill them.

But more than satisfying my desire for external achievement, the challenges of business have grown my character more than any other aspect of my adult life. My career has been the crucible for the formation of my soul.

The pain of interpersonal and business challenges has caused me to cry out to God in my trouble. Though I have often prayed for God to deliver me *from* my circumstances, more often he has delivered me *through* my circumstances. Through my honesty with God, he has drawn me into an ever-deeper intimacy with him.

God does this in small, daily ways. He performs archaeological digs on the feelings that emerge from the day-to-day activities of business. These investigations reveal invisible infrastructures of sloppy theology, thickets of hidden motives, and subterranean reservoirs of unreleased emotion preventing me from living into the freedom he's designed for us.

Business has exposed my fears, and God has set me free from them. My nervousness before board meetings (*pre-meeting syndrome,* or "PMS" as I affectionately call it) has revealed an unhealthy need to prove myself.

Only God can liberate us from our fears and our faults. He does this in small ways, but sometimes he does it in dramatic ways.

The biggest failure of my life came through a large-scale telecommunications start-up in Brazil. After winning the license to compete with the incumbent phone company, we raised $2.5 billion and hired four thousand people in two years to build out wireless communication services to eighty cities covering 125 million people across the country. The company accelerated into the fastest-growing company of its kind in the world, putting on half a million customers in the first ten months. The stock price tripled. And then . . . one of our partners decided to exit their international operations, leaving a $100 million hole in the business plan. The capital markets crashed, curtailing our plans to go public, and we saw some cracks emerging in the operations. With the spiral accelerating, I was drafted by the shareholders to move to Brazil and take over the reins as CEO.

Shortly after I arrived, we discovered the operations were in even worse shape than I had expected. Forty percent of our customers couldn't pay their bills. As my bodyguard pulled our bulletproof car into the underground parking garage every morning, I felt like I was going to throw up. I was forced to lay off fifteen hundred people to save twenty-five hundred jobs. We restructured the billions of dollars in debt. We raised another $260 million from our shareholders and ultimately sold the company, but the investors lost a majority of their investment.

Yet the pain of this business failure paled in comparison to the spiritual anguish it wrought in my soul. It took this massive failure to reveal that I had made achievement my god. I would not have recognized achievement in its form as a golden calf, formed through decades of striving, had it not been unveiled by the pain of this business failure.

The fiery trials of business remove the base alloys from our souls, purifying and softening us so God can mold us into the shape that seems best to him. Great joy, newfound freedom, and lasting peace are the residues of the white-hot refining fire of divine love.

FOR REFLECTION

- Call to mind a situation from your career that has caused or is causing you significant pain. Then imagine yourself responding to this pain in two different ways: avoidance and immersion.

- In the first instance, how does it leave you feeling to avoid the pain, to wish it weren't there, to hope it would go away?

- Next, submit fully to the pain. How might God want to refine you through this pain?

- In fact, go beyond the pain to death. What part of yourself might need to die through this suffering? Is there a part of you that is raised into fuller life as a result of this fire of divine love doing its work in your soul?

6

BETTER PEOPLE AT WORK

*Whoever wants to become great among you
must be your servant, and whoever wants
to be first must be slave of all. For even the Son
of Man did not come to be served, but to serve,
and to give his life as a ransom for many.*

MARK 10:43-45

> *As we are set free to more fully experience
> God's love, we will more fully love those
> he has placed in our care.*

What if we came to see the purpose of business as helping people flourish by loving and serving them, rather than simply making a profit? We will never fully redeem the world of business, but as we give ourselves to Christ, perhaps we can become the change we hope to see.

Surrendering to Christ makes us better employees. Imagine the benefit to the organizations we serve if we showed up at work with purified motivations and a genuine humility. What if everything we thought about regarding our work, and everything we did for the sake of our work, advanced the cause of the organization instead of seeking to advance ourselves?

As we surrender to Christ, God breathes his Spirit into us, and the Spirit then flows through us into our work and onto others. As we come emptied of personal ambition, the need to be right, and our innate craving for the applause of others, we are free to do the work to which we are called. As we live from this place, won't we more fully live up to the economic, moral, and even spiritual contract between us and the one who signs our paycheck?

Surrendering to Christ makes us better bosses. I once was talking with the owner of a large business who mentioned that his father had been a pastor. The business owner commented, "My congregation is bigger than his was."

I had to smile.

Peter tells us, "Care for the flock that God has entrusted to you" (1 Peter 5:2 NLT). Perhaps as we consider the flock (employees) under our care, not paternalistically or maternalistically but pastorally, we might focus less on the task and more on the people. And as we do, we might accomplish the tasks just as successfully while leaving people feeling cared for and more whole.

And as our team grows in their capabilities, we can become less and they can become more. Doesn't authentic leadership leave a chorus of people proclaiming, "We did it ourselves!"? And they would be right.

Surrendering to Christ makes us better coworkers. As we live in a posture of surrender, our coworkers will notice that we are focused on doing the right thing rather than doing the right thing for ourselves. And the joy we unknowingly express by our countenance will be contagious and attractive to others.

Becoming more surrendered to God, won't we also forge relationships with our coworkers in bonds of authenticity that keep us from filling our gunnysacks with resentment? Trust becomes the source of courage to speak our minds in meetings and to confront the inevitable differences that arise between us, knowing we will be right with one another on the other side of the conflict. In committed relationships, we toast to what we could not have accomplished separately but have achieved together.

A company whose workers are united in a bond of mutual trust, who face in the same direction with their eyes focused on common goals, will surely accomplish much more, and have more fun along the way, than one whose people are warring with one another.

Of course, this is the ideal. There is likely to be as much broken glass in our relationships in the workplace as there is champagne spilled out of cups that runneth over with the joy of working together. But as for me and the people I lead, I'd rather live a life that is aspirational and positive than one that is apathetic and cynical.

Jesus' "new command" is that we love one another as he has loved us. That is a tall order impossible to achieve under our own power. But the God who fills the vacuum created by our surrender—like the expanding diaphragm fills the lungs with air—can breathe his love into others through us, whatever our role at work, at home, or in the world.

FOR REFLECTION

- How might you go about your work differently in each of the following roles at work?
- As an employee:

  How might you think about the "spiritual contract" between you and your employer? What should be expected of you? What should you expect of them?
- As a coworker:

  What would it be like if you loved (I mean, really loved) your coworkers the way God loves us? How would the Christ in you love "the least of these" in them the way he loves "the least of these" in you? What if you loved your neighbor in the next cubicle the way you love yourself, as Christ loves you?
- As a boss:

  How might your leadership change if your deepest desire was to see your employees grow into the full expression of themselves, instead of viewing them as a means of achieving your or the company's goals?

7

SURRENDERED LEADERSHIP

He must become greater; I must become less.

JOHN 3:30

> **As we become less and Jesus becomes more in us, we will lead as his followers.**

Surrender is the first stone our toes touch on the path toward God, and each moment asks this same relinquishment of us. As we submit ourselves and our wills to God, he begins to occupy his proper place within us, until it is no longer we who live but Christ who lives in us. And as he leads us, he will lead others through us. John the Baptist is a model in this.

John was a celebrity in his day. Immense crowds came out to see him, so much so that the king worried that John might lead a rebellion. But when Jesus came—the one for whom John had been making straight the way, the one whose sandals John was not worthy to remove, the Bridegroom for whom John was merely the groomsman—John was more than ready to lead from the second chair. "He must become greater," John said; "I must become less."

John's followers may have had trouble seeing it, but by placing himself beneath Jesus, John was doing what was best for them. The focus had to shift from *preparation* to *actualization* of God's plan of salvation. And that meant placing Jesus in the spotlight.

As John shrank so that Jesus might grow, we likewise are called to yield our puny plans to Jesus' agenda for our lives. It took me seven years, through my late twenties, to realize that I was looking through this telescope from the wrong end: I was trying to fit God into my plans instead of submitting myself to his plan. A week after this realization, I submitted my life to Jesus on that run around the lake, though my surrender dripped with the residual reluctance of my strong will rather than exuding the fragrance of John's gracious submission.

Over time, this initial act of surrender has led me to take positions with companies that had lost their way and to others requiring a comprehensive turnaround—financially, operationally, strategically, and reputationally. In part, I said yes to these roles out of a desire to see whether these principles and this prototype we have in Jesus would stand up to the heat of the kitchen. They have. And in the cases where I failed externally, God has grown me internally.

Sometimes big change masquerades as small change. We go to the meetings as we are directed by our electronic calendars, but we increasingly see these commitments and our to-do lists as God's call on our time as we develop these priorities in prayer. Seen from the outside, what we do may change little or not at all, but *how* we do what we do and *why* we do what we do are radically altered as we come to view every moment as a sacrament.

Surrendered leadership leads us into freedom. We might find ourselves freer to constructively speak our mind in a conversation, bound more by a desire to move the discussion forward than by a straitjacket of concern about how we will be received by others. We might view the "walk-in business" as less of an interruption and more of an opportunity to respond to the needs of others that emerge in the course of the day. I might be more inclined to ask my executive assistant about her weekend, or be as genuinely interested in my colleague's son who broke his arm playing lacrosse as in the quality of the financial analysis I'd asked her to perform.

Surrender to God does not leave us floating in purposeless irrelevance. It brings focus and meaning. God knows we have work to do during the course of our days. He asks us to work, just as he is always at his work. But now our work takes on greater importance and meaning, for God's work becomes our work.

Jesus understands the pressure of the demands on our lives because of the demands he experienced during his life. The needs of the people were endless, and the requests of the crowds were relentless.

Once he sent his apostles out to do the work he commanded, and while they were gone he learned the bitter news that Herod had beheaded John the Baptist. Jesus must have been deeply bereaved. "Then, because so many people were coming and going that they did not even have a chance to eat, he said to [his disciples], 'Come with me by yourselves to a quiet place and get some rest'" (Mark 6:31).

But when the boat arrived on the other side of the lake, the crowds were waiting for them. "When Jesus landed and saw a large crowd, he had compassion on them, because they were like sheep without a shepherd" (v. 34). I would not have had compassion on them. I would have been impatient with them, frustrated that they had broken into my time of rest. I would have thought I deserved time to grieve my deceased friend and forerunner. It is a testimony to Jesus' character that, even in his exhaustion, he considered the needs of others more than his own. Even under pressure, his perspective and his purpose were unwavering.

In April 2018, the world learned about Southwest flight 1380, whose left engine exploded, causing the cabin to decompress and putting the passengers in mortal danger. Nearing the airport for an emergency landing, the pilot, Tammy Jo Shults, grasped for what to do. It was then that the cockpit recorder captured her saying, "Heavenly Father?" And when she landed, "Thank you, Lord. Thank you, thank you, Lord." Prayer had long been an integral part of Tammy Jo's life. She learned a key lesson through this experience: under pressure, habits become instincts.

Surrendered leadership doesn't universally prescribe that we always be focused or relaxed, tough-minded or tenderhearted, compassionate or demanding. Jesus exhibited all of these attributes during his stay with us on earth. The surrendered life is not servitude to a set of precepts but submission to a person who is our example and who is with us in every circumstance of our lives. As we grow into deeper relationship with him, his desires become our desires. His instincts become our instincts. His compassion becomes our compassion.

As Jesus increases and we decrease, our will is increasingly united with God's will, and his will is done on earth as it is in heaven. This is his plan for the world and a great source of joy in ours.

FOR REFLECTION

- Can you recall an instance where you surrendered to God and felt his leading? What was the impact of his leadership—on you and on the part of the world you touch?
- In what part of your work life might Jesus be calling you to trust and follow him today?

PART 2

TRANSFORMED

LEARNING NEW WAYS OF THINKING AND BEING

• • •

*God seeks to transform every element of our being
so that our whole mind, heart, and soul will be filled
with him who is love. Our careers can become the
crucible for the formation of our souls as God uses
our work to do his work in us.*

8

A PROGRESSION OF SELVES

You were taught, with regard to your
former way of life, to put off your old self,
which is being corrupted by its deceitful desires;
to be made new in the attitude of your minds;
and to put on the new self, created to be like
God in true righteousness and holiness.

EPHESIANS 4:22-24

> ### *God rescues our true self from*
> ### *the bondage of our false self.*

The genius of God's design is that he accomplishes his work in our souls and in the world simultaneously, and he does it through the ordinary circumstances of our lives. Every moment conspires to bring us into deeper intimacy with him and invites us to join him in accomplishing his work in this world.

I'm grateful that he uses incomplete people to move his work toward completion. He asks, seeks, and knocks at the door, wanting to transform us that he might transform the world through us. That he would long to return both us and the world to his divine design reveals a self-emptying love beyond our comprehension.

Early in my career, and in the newness of my conversion, my self-talk was characterized by a "when, then" mentality: *When I receive more responsibility, then I can make a real impact.* And in the spiritual dimension: *When I am purified by God, then I can be an instrument of his will.* Thankfully I was not always prone to the procrastination this mindset created.

Shortly after I came to a surrendered faith in Christ, I was having lunch with a senior engineering colleague in our company. He was a slender young man with a well-trimmed beard, a brilliant mind, and a quick wit. We'd bonded through building a start-up company together (and through the nine holes of golf we played with a group of coworkers most Tuesday summer evenings). At one point in our lunchtime discussion, we got into the deeper things of life—faith and purpose.

"To me, it's all about being a good person," he said.

I didn't agree, but I wasn't sure I should contradict him.

Finally I cautiously said, "Being good is certainly important, but I don't think it's the foundation for a life of deeper meaning. What really matters is whether we are going to live our life for God or for ourselves."

We remained friends during the years we worked together but then lost touch as our careers diverged. About ten years later, this familiar face came rushing up to me at the top of the escalator in an airport. My old friend seemed as delighted to see me as I was to see him.

"I never forgot our lunch discussion those many years ago," he said. "I reflected on it for a long time, and I eventually concluded you were right—the core issue is living our lives for God and not ourselves." He was effusive in telling me about how his life had been transformed by his surrender to Christ.

I was glad I hadn't held back from sharing my newfound conclusion to him during that lunch as thirty-year-olds. If I'd concluded that I had to wait in order to be qualified to discuss matters of faith, the opportunity would have been permanently deferred. And I would have missed out on the beautiful experience of seeing the ripple effects of one conversation spoken out of my own vulnerability.

God's way is to use us along the way even as we're still on the way. Telling our team, "This point in our strategic plan is unclear to me," can lead to a discussion that clarifies our thinking and deepens our conviction about the direction we should go. Apologizing to an employee for the way I behaved in a meeting can deepen the bonds of trust.

I have tasted the intimacy with God for which we were designed, but it has not been permanent. I have seen the progress he has made in my soul, but so much more remains to be done. While he is liberating us from our bondage to decay, I spend most of my time at the tip of the blade where he is prying my true self from the bondage of the false self, held fast by an adhesive of hideous strength.

Perhaps it's only natural, as one recovering from decades of pursuing the god of achievement, that I am much more aware of what's left to be done than what's been done. Thank you, Peter, for showing us that inexpressible and glorious joy comes as we "are receiving" (not after we *have* received) the goal of our faith (1 Peter 1:8-9). Joy does not remain outside the door until the house is completely tidy.

Since we disobeyed in the Garden of Eden, we have been propping up the old man (or, of course, woman) within us, who can only live a hollow, unfulfilled life. Yet our faith strips us of our old selves, enabling us to live into and out of our true selves. This new self acts with purified motives. We are more objective. We are more fully present to the people and issues in front of us as we are less distracted by the noise of the world around us.

Arrogance, and all the other manifestations of that insidious pride, colors our judgment without our even knowing that the crayons have been pulled out of the box. As we increasingly understand that our meaning comes from knowing we are loved, we strive less to artificially derive meaning from status, recognition, or praise.

God has searched us and he knows us. God wants to reveal our true selves to us. Thomas Merton famously concluded that to become holy is to become ourselves. Surrender doesn't deprive us of who we are; it leads us into who we truly are.

As we are emptied of our old selves, Christ is free to become himself in us. We think more like him, act more like him, become more like him. Perhaps as we look in a mirror down the path of life, we will see the shrewdness of snakes and the innocence of doves even as we live as sheep among wolves.

The freedom and joy we experience, as our true selves arrive more fully at our desks in the morning, will be contagious and attractive to others. People enjoy being with people who are comfortable in their own skin. As I more fully surrender myself to Jesus, the organization I serve will flourish by the presence of my absence that allows God to be present.

FOR REFLECTION

- Imagine yourself looking in a mirror and seeing two versions of yourself—your old, shadow self and your new, growing self.
- What are the qualities you see in each of these selves? Do the faces look different from each other as you gaze at this reflected image through the eyes of faith?
- Where is God currently at work, growing the one and reducing the other as he transforms you more and more into the likeness of his Son?

9

LIFE AS A CLASSROOM

I will instruct you and teach you in
the way you should go;
I will counsel you with my loving eye on you.

PSALM 32:8

> *Life is a classroom. We are the students.*
> *God is the teacher. And the core curriculum*
> *is to grow us into the character of Christ.*

Some years ago, as a recently hired CFO, I made my first trip to Japan as part of a broader tour through Asia to review the budgets of our regional operations. I ate sushi that qualified as a work of art and outrageously expensive Wagyu beef that melted in my mouth (thank you, investment bankers). As I entered my micro-room at the Shiba Park Hotel, the bathroom was a foot away from the door, but I couldn't find the shower. Then I looked up and saw the shower nozzle coming out of the wall. The bathroom *was* the shower. I was loving my first taste of Japan and the creativity and inventiveness around me.

Yet none of this prepared me for what happened in the crammed conference room during the budget meeting the next morning. The country leadership team was building a successful business, and the rapid growth made it challenging to forecast. The president of international sales, an American, thought the Japanese team's goals weren't aggressive enough, while the Japanese leadership attempted to defend their conservative budget. A normal business discussion disintegrated into a biting argument.

During my prayer time the next morning, with my outstretched legs nearly spanning my hotel room, I came across Paul's writing to the Galatians. "The entire law is fulfilled in keeping this one command: 'Love your neighbor as yourself.' If you bite and devour each other, watch out or you will be destroyed by each other" (Galatians 5:14-15).

I wondered what a business would look like if its people lived by this command.

If every moment is a classroom in miniature, this was an important learning opportunity for me. Were there lessons embedded in the acrimony of that conference room? Could I have done more to ensure that our leaders were supporting one another rather than devouring one another? Could God's principles have been transported from the pages of my Bible into that conversation in the conference room?

We ultimately established the more aggressive budgets, but not without the local managers being left with scars from the trampling hooves of their superiors running roughshod over them. We missed an opportunity to openly and objectively discuss how we might have bridged a divide created by differences in perspective and cultures.

I've since learned to look for God's will and his word embedded in every moment of my life. He has a point of view for how we should act, and especially for who we should be, in virtually every circumstance.

The many hours we will work in our lifetime make our work one of the best places for the Master Teacher to do his work in us. Not because it's easy, but because it's hard. I often say, "Where two or more are gathered, there will be challenges." If we are in conflict, or confused, or stymied, we can ask ourselves, "What are the benefits of this struggle?" Surely God's lessons are embedded in these experiences.

Even in the midst of my struggles, I was beginning to see difficulties, not as getting in the way of life, but *as* the way of life. In fact, embracing our difficulties is the way *to* life. Thérèse de Lisieux, the nineteenth-century Carmelite nun, said that the path to holiness is fidelity in the small things. This perspective provides a healthy shift for this innate perfectionist.

Once we have surrendered to God we become as little children, and like children, we go to school. We begin learning how God wants us to live, in our families, in our work, and in the world around us. As we do, we begin to be transformed from people who are following our own blueprint for happiness to those who are living by God's design—and becoming people of greater joy and influence because of it.

No school bell rings when a God lesson is about to begin. But as the proverb says, "When the pupil is ready, the teacher will appear." As we develop eyes to see and ears to hear, we will begin to learn what the Master has come to teach.

FOR REFLECTION

- Recall two to four times from your past where you now see that God was teaching you. What were God's lesson plans for you in those moments? How deeply did you learn those lessons? Or are they still part of his curriculum for you?
- Can you catch a glimpse of his current lesson plan for you? What's your attitude toward the instruction?

10

THE SINE OF THE TIMES

I have learned to be content
whatever the circumstances.

PHILIPPIANS 4:11

> **The ups and downs of life aren't a problem**
> **to be fixed but a reality to be embraced.**

In *The Screwtape Letters*, by C. S. Lewis, a senior devil instructs a junior devil about human beings: "Their bodies, passions, and imaginations are in continual change, for to be in time means to change. Their nearest approach to constancy, therefore, is undulation—the repeated return to a level from which they repeatedly fall back, a series of troughs and peaks."

This law of undulation certainly describes my own experience, and probably yours too. We have highs and lows. Our feelings ebb and flow, often even more dramatically than our circumstances.

It seems we are destined to live *within* these inescapable undulations of life, but how should we live *with* them?

I know what I have done. During the highs, I've taken credit. During the lows, I've taken over.

At the highs, I've become god. At the lows, I've blamed God. In the mid-zone, I've probably forgotten God.

When our company has exceeded Wall Street expectations, and its stock price zooms up 25 percent in one day, I am tempted to bask in the euphoria rather than falling on my knees in gratitude. When the challenges of turning around a business prove to be even more difficult than I imagined, I am inclined to suck it up, buck up, and double down on my drive to fix the problems rather than remembering that apart from Jesus I can do nothing.

But what does God think about this?

I have come to believe that God invites us to deepen our relationship with him through the highs *and* the lows.

The apostle James opened his letter with a dramatic admonition to his readers to see their circumstances in exactly the opposite way from how I have often lived mine. "Consider it pure joy, my brothers and sisters, whenever you face trials of many kinds, because you know that the testing of your faith produces perseverance. Let perseverance finish its work so that you may be mature and complete, not lacking anything" (James 1:2-4).

All of life, even (or perhaps particularly) suffering, is designed to shape our character so that we might come into a more complete and perfect union with God. When it is hardest to listen, we must listen the hardest. When we find people hardest to love, we learn to love the most. When God appears to be absent, he may be more present than ever. John of the Cross, the sixteenth-century Spanish mystic, observed that these times of apparent darkness may actually be temporary blindness as we are engulfed in God's overwhelming light.

Viewed through the eyes of faith, our malcontentedness can go from a source of frustration to an opportunity for prayer. If we are out of sorts with the world, we are probably out of whack with God. The ebbs of our undulation can reveal the false gods and worldly desires that prevent us from deepening our relationship with the only source of true peace.

Furthermore, when the troubles of this world meet our spiritual retinas, we can be freed from our fears. A sinking in the cycle of undulation can become a wonderful thing because it is an indication there is some kind of underlying issue (an anxiety, an inappropriate worldview, a facet of my sinful nature) that, if understood and addressed, will contribute to my wholeness. I'm not helpless. As I cooperate with the unchanging God, he grows the Spirit of Christ in me, even if my difficult circumstances do not change.

Our lives will undulate. Our health, our relationships, our success on the job, our energy level, our passion for God, our moods—they all cycle upward and downward over time. We're each in our own little boat riding the waves of our circumstances and emotions.

It's pointless to try to smooth out the sea. The fullness of life is experienced by riding the waves at their highs and their lows. Contentment comes from the company in our boat, not the circumstances through which our boat travels. The joy of the journey comes from being in the company of Christ, traveling with an ever-improving version of ourselves, and sharing the experience with people we enjoy and respect.

FOR REFLECTION

- How has God shaped you through the undulations of your life? Having persevered through these challenges, how are you a more complete person than you were?
- What kind of traveling companion have you found Jesus to be?

11

GO FAST OR GO DEEP

*The kingdom of heaven is like yeast that
a woman took and mixed into about sixty pounds
of flour until it worked all through the dough.*

MATTHEW 13:33

> **While we may desire speed of change, God is
> more interested in depth of change. He wants
> to transform the very substance of our being.**

In *The Practice of the Presence of God*, Brother Lawrence—a cook in
a Parisian monastery during the 1600s—wrote of an overzealous
friend, "[Our dear sister] seems so full of goodwill, but she wants to
go faster than grace allows. It is not possible to become spiritually
mature all at once."

I have been this "dear sister." It takes time to learn to stay in the
place of grace and to go at the pace of grace. I am a man of momentum. I am committed, even driven, to become a better person. I
want to be better next month than I am this month, and better next
year than this year.

As the saying goes, God loves us just the way we are and too much
to leave us as we are, so in this sense my interests are aligned with
God's. Both of us want to see me change. Yet God and I have often had
very different views of what the process of change should look like.

I am ready to move on before I've really learned the lessons God has for me. He wants to produce lasting change in me, while I draw back from the heat of the refining fire of divine love, hoping the trials won't last. I'm like an antsy child who can't sit still long enough to allow God to plumb the depths of my being. Perhaps I'm afraid of what he will see. Or even more, afraid of what *I* might see. In other words . . .

I want to go fast.

God wants to go deep.

There are times when God changes something miraculously overnight, but in my experience that's not how he normally works in shaping our character and spiritual maturity. God seems more inclined to simmer us in a slow cooker than to quick fry us in a wok. Rapid change leaves us raw and unchanged on the inside. God wants to improve us in lasting ways. He works on root causes, not superficial symptoms, and he keeps going until he transforms the very nature of our nature.

And in these times when the pace of the world is accelerating, it is doubly important for our character as leaders to be formed deeply enough to keep up with the speed and challenges facing the organizations we lead.

Airplane wings produce lift because of the shape of the wing—the air flowing across the top of the wing has to travel farther, and therefore faster, than the air flowing under the wing. It's called Bernoulli's principle. The greater the speed, the less pressure exerted on the surface over which the air is traveling. When we travel through life too fast, we are avoiding the pressure that will mold us into the shape that seems best to God.

Indeed, the kingdom of heaven is like leaven that slowly works its way through a lump of dough.

The Catholic version of the Nicene Creed proclaims a belief in Jesus who is "*consubstantial* with the Father." I had to look up that four-syllable word. It means "to be made of the same substance." God transforms our human nature to be more like his divine nature. Selfishness is turned into selflessness. God is love. He wants to make us into love. I have participated in board meetings essentially every quarter for the past forty years. I can easily remember the most painful one of them all. In God's providence, it would become the crucible through which he would shape me more fully into this love.

Some months before this particular board meeting, I had discussed with the CEO the importance of putting the right leaders in the right roles to maximize our collective success. Coming out of these often-challenging discussions, he agreed that, among other changes taking place, I would be promoted to a higher-level executive role. Problem solved—I thought! (That was my "go fast" mistake.) Surely the board would give perfunctory approval to the change.

I was very wrong.

During the meeting, one board member questioned the proposed new leadership structure. "Who is really going to be in charge?" he demanded. The tension escalated, resulting in a shouting match and name-calling around the table.

And that wasn't the worst of it. In the hallway immediately following this explosion, another board member reamed me out personally. He thought I was making a power play.

I have always been someone who deeply values harmony in relationships, so these biting and untrue comments cut me to the core. I didn't care about the title I was receiving. I cared about the company's success. I spent a tearful afternoon walking along the paths through our neighborhood, trying to make sense of it all.

The next morning I went back to speak with the founder, suggesting that we try to sort things out between the two of us. We spent the next couple of days discussing our respective roles and eventually reached a resolution. We would go on to work together for another two years.

As much as I wanted to escape the pain, God wanted me to fully embrace the pain so that he might shape me in more important and lasting ways ("go deep"). By staying in the tension, I learned two things. First, I learned to be more direct. I experienced firsthand the importance of not sugarcoating comments out of deference for a relationship. This superficial, distorted understanding of kindness prevents the painful conversation often required to expose and deal with underlying issues. And I learned forgiveness. Real, practical, gut-wrenching forgiveness. How hard it is for the wounded to forgive the wounder. It would require putting to death my desire for retaliation or withdrawal.

I'm a more complete human being because of God's deep work, in spite of my desire to avoid the pain that produces progress. I wouldn't have chosen it and couldn't have done it on my own.

Being in relationship with Jesus and knowing "he is with us always" is at the heart of our transformation as much as it was for his apostles. "When they saw the courage of Peter and John and realized that they were unschooled, ordinary men, they were astonished and they took note that these men *had been with Jesus*" (Acts 4:13, emphasis added).

Throughout Scripture, and throughout history, we see that God has shaped his people through years and decades of following him and being with him. As we rededicate ourselves to God—at work, at home, at church, out and about in the world—he who began a good work in us will bring it to completion. And the change is wrought at the heart of our being.

FOR REFLECTION

- Have there been times when you have been traveling so fast through life that you haven't allowed, or have purposefully avoided, the work God wants to do in you? Can you revisit those times now and allow God to continue to work his yeast all through the dough of your soul?

■ Conversely, have there been times when you did slow down, when you stayed with the questions, when you paused to listen? How has God shaped you through these experiences?

12

DRIVEN BY FEAR
OR LED BY LOVE?

There is no fear in love.
But perfect love drives out fear.

1 JOHN 4:18

> ### *Fear imprisons us. Love sets us free.*

This side of perfection, we are all plagued with fears. Throughout my career, some of my greatest hits have included

- fear of insignificance
- fear of failing at my job
- fear of not being understood or accepted by others
- fear of not having enough money
- fear of failing to achieve my potential

When I feel ashamed of my fears, I take solace from the people in Scripture who have been afraid. David, the mighty warrior and king, exclaimed that God "delivered me from all my fears"—an admission that he had fears in the first place (Psalm 34:4). The angel Gabriel, after telling Mary she was "highly favored" and the Lord was with her, said, "Do not be afraid, Mary" (Luke 1:28, 30). And how often did Jesus tell his disciples, "Do not be afraid"?

Fear is natural enough for us humans. And it is not always bad. Fear pushes us to run from bears that would eat us alive . . . and from people or situations that might do the same thing.

Nevertheless, fear is usually a bad motivator. At least I know that I have been pushed in harmful directions by my own silent but powerful fears. My fear of insignificance, for example, has driven me to try to fill this interior vacuum with external achievements. And that is just exhausting.

I have long been familiar with 1 John 4:18, but to me this verse has often been a mere idea, not a personal reality. While I don't always live the truth of this Scripture, I am coming to see how love and fear can be competing motivations.

Fear drives us. Love draws us.

Answering Jesus' call to "Come, follow me" leads us into the only perfect love capable of driving out fear. He is safe. We can come to him when we are weary and burdened, and we will find rest. In the world we will have trouble, but in him we can find peace.

Because both fear and love produce movement, they can look similar on the outside. To others, it might appear as a high level of energy or motivation. But it feels dramatically different on the inside to be driven by fear versus running toward love.

Fear imprisons me. Love sets me free.

Fear squelches my expression as a person. Love releases it.

Fear is a barrier between God and me. Love connects us.

I have been motivated by both at different times in my life. In fact, my motivations are rarely pure. It seems I'm destined to live with both carrots and sticks in my knapsack this side of heaven.

When I was thirty-five years old and the recently named CFO of a public company, I attended my first investor conference, in Monterey, California. I'd turned the hotel room chair to face out the window to pray, but the calm of the sea outside my window could not calm the fear within me. The following interior conversational prayer ensued.

Why am I afraid? I asked myself.

This answer came, *I am being paid all this money to represent the company well. I want to do a good job.*

Why does that cause me to be afraid?

Well, what if an investor asks me a question I can't answer?

Okay, but what is the connection between the desire to do a good job and the fear that produces?

I don't want to look incompetent.

Why does it bother me to be perceived as incompetent?

I was beginning to see. *So it's pride, isn't it?*

Underlying the fear was pride seeking to prop up an image, an image of competency. Tearfully, I wrote this confession in my journal: "Yes, the source of my fear is pride."

Having this conversation in the safety of the pure love of Jesus helped me see the connection between fear and pride. Paradoxically, as this truth became clear, I went from being imprisoned by fear to being set free by love.

The antidote to fear is love.

FOR REFLECTION

- Allow yourself to enter into a strong negative emotion you are currently feeling. Sit with it. Try not to manipulate, justify, or explain it. Simply be with it for a few minutes.

- Now, perform an archaeological dig to get beneath these feelings. Why do you feel this way? Are these reasons valid as you imagine them to be viewed by God, or do they reveal some aspect of your thinking or character that he might like to nudge closer to his likeness?

- If some underlying spiritual infrastructure is revealed through this reflection and prayer, how can this truth begin to set you free?

13

CALMING
THE STORMS WITHIN

*[Jesus] got up, rebuked the wind and said
to the waves, "Quiet! Be still!" Then the wind
died down and it was completely calm.*

MARK 4:39

> **God rebukes the source of our unrest to bring
> us into the peace that can only come from him.**

For all its excitement and potential, the world of business can also be
a ball of anxiety. Entrepreneurs are kept up at night worrying about
whether their fledgling companies will survive. What will happen to
their investment if the gamble fails? Our commitment to do our best
drives us to work long hours, leading to burnout and visits to the
doctor's office. Some of us have specific triggers for our fears, such as
public speaking, negotiating with an important client, or having a
difficult conversation with an underperforming employee.

As we surrender ourselves to God and savor even a few delicious
morsels of intimacy with him, we are brought into a feeling of com-
pleteness, wholeness, and peace. This place—beyond our intellect,
on the other side of reason, not manufactured by us but given by
God—is a garden of divine tranquility. As God brings us through this

transformation, we can experience profound contentment, needing nothing but him alone.

One way I find it helpful to pray is by inserting myself into the stories of Scripture. I like to read the story of Jesus calming the storm in Mark 4:35-41 by imaginatively adding myself to the crew of disciples in that fishing boat.

Not long after we leave the stability of the shore, the wind whips the water into frightening waves. In our fear, we awaken Jesus from his peaceful sleep, crying above the din of the wind, "Don't you care if we drown?"

He gets up, rebukes the wind, and says to the waves, "Quiet! Be still!" Notice Jesus doesn't rebuke the waves; he rebukes the wind, which is the source of the waves. Jesus addresses the cause, not just the symptoms. And as he does, the wind dies down and the rough sea becomes completely calm.

The Spirit of Jesus within us similarly rebukes the causes of our restlessness, our worry, and our anxiety. Calm comes to the water of our souls as Jesus exercises his authority over the winds that disturb the stillness within us.

Time and again, he has met me in the anxiousness before a big presentation, in my fears that the turnaround will not be successful, in dealing with VDPs (Very Difficult People, as my friend calls them), and in the stress of not knowing what to do or from having too much to do. Through these opportunities to turn to Jesus and trust him, I can ultimately proclaim with the psalmist, "It was good for me to be afflicted" (Psalm 119:71).

FOR REFLECTION

■ Try inserting yourself into the scene of the storm on the lake. Then imagine that this scene is occurring within you. What winds might be howling and waves roiling within you right now?

- Imagine Jesus rebuking the wind and saying to the waves within you, "Quiet! Be still!"

- Perhaps you could try speaking these words of Jesus to yourself in a voice that seems appropriate to you. And now repeat these words . . . again . . . and again . . . in an ever-softer voice. Let the words become your mantra. Repeat them until the words become your feelings.

- Can you feel yourself growing calmer? Can you experience the presence of Jesus?

- As you emerge from this prayer, do you find yourself wanting to express your gratitude to Jesus?

- Speak to Jesus now as one friend would to another. He is listening.

14

OUR TIME IS NOT OUR TIME

Do not boast about tomorrow,
for you do not know what a day may bring.

PROVERBS 27:1

There is a time for everything,
and a season for every activity under the heavens.

ECCLESIASTES 3:1

> *All of life is an interruption—an interruption*
> *of our agenda by God's.*

Early in my career, many things were wrong in the way I thought about time. I lived too many of my days with the belief that time was for racking up achievements and polishing my résumé, even if it was for the admissions department in heaven. While I have been predisposed to giving my time to activities for the benefit of others since the days of growing up with a sister who had a disability and with parents who modeled selflessness, too often during my earlier years I dedicated myself to these endeavors with a divided heart. Surely I had one eye on the audience and the other on my résumé as I spoke to the legislature during college as the Idaho state president of a teens' organization for citizens with disabilities.

During those years when the idol of achievement was my un-acknowledged but very real god, our pastor preached a sermon on the purpose of time. His central thesis was "Time is for becoming." That is, for becoming more like Jesus. Even as his words stood in contrast to my lived values, they seemed right to me.

In an effort to change my view of time I synthesized some key tenets on a three-by-five-inch card. I carried this dog-eared card in my folio for ten years.

God's view of time.

- Time is a gift from God.

- Time is for becoming.

- The key is to do the right thing at the right time—"a time for everything" (Ecclesiastes 3:1).

- Time will cause us frustration on earth, for we are designed as eternal beings.

- Our time is punctuated by strategic appointments with God.

I wanted to test this final idea that God meets us at strategic points in our lives, so I made a list of times when I believed God entered my life directly and provided direction. Following are a few of those times.

Age twenty-four. Driving by the freeway exit to Black Canyon on my way home from Boise to Weiser, Idaho, I sensed God's clarity and peace over the decision to marry Linda. I "re-proposed" to her, and now for over forty years we have gratefully been partners for life.

Age twenty-nine. I surrendered my life to Jesus. This moment changed the purpose, priorities, and trajectory of my entire life.

Age thirty-five. I was recruited by a former board member of the company where I was president to become CFO of a much larger public company. After five times of trying to own my own business, I realized God had a different idea in mind. He wanted me to live fully for him in the world I couldn't control. I'd been trying to create a world I could control, even if it was for the seemingly noble purpose of owning and operating companies based on God's principles.

Age fifty. Our family felt drawn to walk more intentionally with those living in poverty. This has led us to take more than twenty trips to low-income communities in Central America with our family, Harvard graduate students, and friends. These experiences also laid the foundations for the careers of both of our sons. Mark studied abroad, in part to achieve fluency in Spanish, and became a lawyer, initially serving as a guardian ad litem so he could be the voice for the voiceless. David decided to get an MBA as he saw the power of business analysis in understanding the economics of a home for children who live on the streets in Honduras and, by extension, for business thinking to address the big problems of the world.

My life and the lives in our family have been far richer for our having accepted these invitations from God, even if they were often delivered in well-sealed envelopes that took some effort to open.

Trying to manage our time in our own wisdom will never produce the peace nor yield the fruit that comes from surrendering control of our time to God. Gratefully, he has no reluctance about canceling our plans to replace them with his own. As I see it now, my time is not my time. Like everything else in the universe, our time is under the lordship of Christ.

If our lives are God's to live through us, not ours to live as we please, then interruptions are no longer interruptions if they are what God would have us do in the moment. In fact, all of our life is an interruption—an interruption of our agenda as it is replaced by God's.

Oswald Chambers, in *My Utmost for His Highest,* observes, "What we call the process, God calls the end." Our journey is indeed our destination when we see the journey as being transformed into the likeness of Christ.

FOR REFLECTION

■ Reflecting on the idea that "time is for becoming," who is God asking you to become? Where might he be at work in you to grow you more fully into the character of Christ? Are there things he might be asking you to continue doing, stop doing, or change the way you are doing?

■ Imagine a person who knows you well speaking at your funeral. What would you want them to say about you? Are you living your life in a way that would lead them to say the words you (and God) would want to hear?

15

GOD'S TO-DO LIST

Many are the plans in a person's heart,
but it is the LORD's purpose that prevails.

PROVERBS 19:21

> **The purpose of planning is not to control**
> **the future but to live God's priorities in**
> **the present.**

I am a planner by nature and like to be well organized. My planning orientation has not only landed me as the leader of the strategic planning processes for the companies I've served, but it has also led me to develop a framework by which I systematically organize my own life. I am never far from a to-do list covering the next week and the next year.

Yet as my abandonment to Christ has grown, it has raised questions about how to live fully for God in the dailyness of life: How do I connect my actions in the present moment to my purpose in life? How do I reconcile the idea of surrendering my life to Jesus with my planful nature? In short, how do I connect the daily with the divine?

Reflecting on these kinds of questions has dramatically changed my approach to planning. I now believe that the purpose of planning is not to set goals to be crossed off a list at some future date, but to bring focus to the present moment.

Life is lived not in reaching the milestones but in crossing the miles.

We don't leave our wedding reception and say, "Whew, I guess I've now done the marriage thing." Rather, the wedding is the *beginning* of a marriage. We will spend a lifetime living out that commitment.

Similarly, we don't live for the birth of our son or daughter, but we are overjoyed at their birth as the beginning of a lifelong, life-giving relationship.

This shift in perspective based on the way we actually live has caused a parallel shift from planning my life around goals. I now refer to the points on my to-do list not as *goals* but as *priorities* or *commitments*. As we clarify what is important to us and commit to these priorities, our lives will unfold in the direction of our desires.

We are responsible for the effort, but we often don't control the results. Particularly for those of us working in business, there is much outside of our control—weather for farmers, unforeseen breakthroughs by competitors in technology businesses, regulatory changes in the telecommunications industry. The more deeply we understand and live the truth about what we truly control, the more freely we can live our lives.

This is not to say we abandon priorities easily or break our commitments. If we say we will complete the first draft of our budget by November 1, we should do just that. If we say we'll follow up on customer complaints within twenty-four hours, we should set up systems to ensure this will happen.

In fact, as we live a life abandoned to God, people should have *greater* reason to trust us to come through for them. We will come to plan more and procrastinate less.

Yet, I've also come through an important paradigm shift that has freed me from being flagellated by a to-do list that can easily become a merciless master. It is this: The objective of planning is not to get everything done on our to-do list—achievement-oriented people never will. Rather, the purpose of a to-do list is to prayerfully prepare our priorities so that at the end of a day, a year, or a lifetime, we can affirmatively answer the question *Did I spend my time the way God wanted me to spend my time?*

Though we don't always know God's purposes, we worship a purposeful God. We see momentum in the story of God's people as we read the biblical narrative, and this is also true of the life he gives each of us. The question is whether we trust God enough to submit our lives to him and his purposes, especially when we cannot see them.

Jesus doesn't give us a map; he serves as our guide. So even when we are shrouded in darkness, we still know the Way. And as our life deepens through our relationship with him, we come to understand that "we live by faith, not by sight" (2 Corinthians 5:7).

The corollary to this truth is that we are most alive when we cannot see. Though we often tell ourselves we wish we could see at the beginning how things will turn out in the end, there is a part of us that actually loves not knowing the outcome. Isn't it more fun to watch a football game live than to watch the recording, already knowing who wins? Humans love competing in contests of all kinds. We are made for adventure. Living the story is far more exciting than reading about it in the newspaper the next day.

Of course, the darkness is still scary to us. Yet a soul that has traversed the miles with God can walk ever more comfortably, even without seeing the way, because it knows the Way and learns the light of truth that will lead it into life.

We cannot surrender without trust. We cannot trust without knowing God. And as we come to know him, our mind will be renewed so that we might be able to approve, test, and more completely follow his will for our lives. Even as it shows up on our daily to-do list.

FOR REFLECTION

- Prayerfully develop your to-do list for today.

- Can you see how these priorities might be God's priorities for you today?

- Can you see them as a concrete manifestation of God's call for you?

- Can you make a connection between these activities and your purpose in life?

- Review this list at the end of the day to see which things were crossed off the list. Do you feel like you focused on the right things? How about the "interruptions" that weren't on your list? Did addressing them bring a smile or a grimace to your face? What about to the face of God?

16

GETTING TO NO

The Sabbath was made for people,
not people for the Sabbath.

MARK 2:27 ISV

> *In order to fully give ourselves to God's*
> *purposes, we must go from being mastered*
> *by the demands on our time to being*
> *master over them.*

One winter evening, when our first son, Mark, was six months old, I came home from work with severe chest pains. I thought I was having a heart attack.

Moments after I walked through the door, Linda wisely suggested I head straight for the hospital. Later that evening the doctors released me, assuring me that I was not having a heart attack.

The same thing happened the next night—chest pains, followed by a severe outbreak of hives.

Over the next few weeks, Linda and I discerned that my problem wasn't heart disease. It was stress.

Before we had kids, neither Linda nor I minded working sixty to eighty hours a week. We wanted to invest ourselves in our careers. (Linda was a successful financial leader, working for Hewlett-Packard for the last ten years of her career. I thought it was great that she made more money than I did for most of the years she was working.) But after Mark was born, and after working part time for a year, our priorities had shifted. Linda decided to redefine motherhood in a way that worked for her to be at home with our kids. I no longer wanted to be at the office in the evenings; I wanted to be home with our son.

The way I was spending my time was not the way I wanted to be spending my time, and this incongruence was the source of the chest pains.

Once I recognized the root of the problem, I committed to fixing it. I had to gain control of my time, because it was clear that the demands on my time were controlling me. The demands of my life had to be wrenched from their position as master over me.

"The Sabbath was made for people, not people for the Sabbath." With these words, Jesus clarified the role of master and slave when it comes to the hierarchy of time.

We cannot give away what is not ours. My time was not my own, because I was owned by it. I was not in a position to give myself wholly to God in those days.

The painful lessons taught by our six-month-old son (who is now in his thirties and with whom I have a cherished relationship) grew into a foundation for our lives. As a new father, I wanted to spend time with our son. I was committed to being a fully engaged dad.

Out of that experience, Linda and I decided what constituted balance for me and, in turn, for our family:

- praying an hour a day
- exercising at least three days a week
- working fifty to fifty-five hours a week
- traveling less than 30 percent of the time

- minimizing evening meetings so we could have dinner together as a family
- limiting my involvement on outside boards to no more than
  two at a time

Though we found ourselves having to be bulldogs with our time
in the early years of establishing these boundaries, they eventually
grew into a natural rhythm, even as we had a second child and the
professional demands on our time grew. We came to experience the
freedom of discipline as our yes became yes and our no could
remain no.

To paraphrase Stephen Covey, it's easier to say no if we have a
stronger yes burning inside of us. Saying yes to God and to our family
has made it easier for me to say no to a world that would enslave me
to its insatiable demands.

FOR REFLECTION

- Are there parts of your life that are controlling you when you'd
  be better off being more in control of them? Perhaps you can
  make a list of these.
- Would you live a more fulfilling and perhaps even a more successful life by drawing boundaries around your time? Where
  would you draw these boundaries?

17

REVERSING THE FLOW

Whoever believes in me, as Scripture has said,
rivers of living water will flow from within them.

JOHN 7:38

> *Life is designed to be lived from the inside out*
> *rather than from the outside in. Things from*
> *the outside cannot fill us on the inside.*

For years, I bought in to the lie of the world that if I focused on getting my external circumstances right, then I would be right within my heart. And these external things were not bad things; they were good things—a wife I loved and who loved me, a good job, enriching friendships, and a house in a neighborhood with a log fort in the backyard and friends for our kids. But over time I began to realize the truth that these externalities, even the good things, could never settle the disquiet at the center of my being.

The lie I was living remained hidden from my sight until God splashed paint on its invisible form. Gradually, I began to see that I had been looking for my work, relationships, and possessions to fill a longing for meaning and contentment that can only be satisfied by God.

I didn't have to look far to see that the mistake I was making was not uncommon to people in positions of leadership.

After moving to Seattle, I came to know a business leader who spoke proudly of the twenty-six boards he was on. At first I was impressed—twenty-six! Then I asked myself, *Why would someone want to be on that many boards?*

As I got to know him more, I could see he felt unfulfilled and insecure. He was trying, perhaps subconsciously, to assuage his feelings of insignificance by associating himself with positions and people of significance.

As I looked in the mirror, I could see I was making the same mistake. I, too, was living my life from the outside in. My error was a difference in degree but not a difference in kind. It didn't work for him, and it wasn't working for me. The silent screams of inadequacy within us cannot be drowned out by the thunder of applause outside us.

Meaning and joy are built not from the outside in but from the inside out. We are designed for God alone to occupy our innermost being. If we are first right with him, then we can be right with the world.

Here's what I have seen at work in my own life. If I'm right with God, then I'm at peace with myself. And if I'm at peace, I can live in harmony with my wife and our two sons. And if I have a harmonious family life, I can give myself wholly to my work for the broader community.

Our essence radiates outward from the core. And in the divine design, God seeks to be the sole occupant on the throne at the core of our being.

Jesus said, "Whoever believes in me, as Scripture has said, rivers of living water will flow from within them" (John 7:38). God's design is for him alone to occupy the throne of our hearts with streams of life-giving water flowing from him at the headwaters of our being, growing the tree of life so that its leaves can be "for the healing of the nations" (Revelation 22:2).

As this emerging perspective began to reorganize the cluttered attic of my mind, it also reoriented the way I viewed my work. I'd searched so hard and so long for meaning from my work, and I'd long sought to change jobs to fill this aching vacuum within. I'd been more focused on changing my circumstances than changing my attitude toward them. In retrospect, it would have been easier to change jobs than to change the person I brought to the job, but it would never have satisfied the ache within.

There are no perfect jobs; there is only a perfect God. Our call is to express this perfect God in the work we are called to do, however imperfectly we might do it. In the end, eight years after surrendering my life to Jesus and after scrawling 350 pages in my journal on finding meaning in my work, I'd changed jobs dramatically . . . without changing business cards.

Rather than thinking about getting the right job, God asks us to think about our job right. As we focus more on the God who fills us up on the inside, we will go about our work on the outside very differently.

FOR REFLECTION

- Contemplate the bi-directional flows you have experienced or may be experiencing in your life.
  - Outside in: Are there things, other than God, that you have used to try to fill a void within you?
  - Inside out: Conversely, can you describe what it is like to be filled with God and to have his Spirit, his love, his compassion flow from you to others?
- What are the residual feelings from living by these opposing flows?

18

TRAVELING COMPANIONS

As iron sharpens iron,
so one person sharpens another.

PROVERBS 27:17

The heartfelt counsel of a friend
is as sweet as perfume and incense.

PROVERBS 27:9 NLT

> ### *Our journey may be our own,*
> ### *but we don't walk it alone.*

I was having lunch with two friends in Seattle a few years ago. Between bites of a cheeseburger, I said, "I want you both to know how grateful I am for our friendship. You have really helped me navigate the challenges of my confusion over meaning in work."

"Thanks," one of them said. "But I think the role of our relationship goes well beyond helping one another get through our challenging circumstances."

"How so?" I asked.

"What if, instead of viewing our relationships as a means of making it through the challenging circumstances of our lives, we saw our circumstances as a means of deepening the relationships in our lives?"

I was intrigued by this inverted perspective. "So this would mean our relationships are the end in themselves."

This exchange led to a seismic shift in my perspective and the way I prioritized my life. I could see that I needed to shift my entire life from a performance orientation to a relational orientation. My relationships with my wife, my family, my friends, and my God were not means to ends but were ends in themselves. Relationships are the fountainhead of our joy.

I received a birthday card one time that said on its cover, "Some people march to the tune of a different drummer . . ." On the inside it said, ". . . but with you the whole band's weird!" As a "corporate mystic" (as my friend Alec describes me), I recognized that there was more than a sliver of truth in that card.

At times I have found it challenging to find friends in faith who connect with the weird band and the deeper levels of my spirituality. Yet, I am a team player and am energized by relationships. And Linda and I have been blessed with many life-giving friendships.

Nor do I want to forget my relationships with the people Linda calls my "dead friends."

When I first read C. S. Lewis's quote "I am the product of . . . endless books," I thought, *So am I!* This recognition prompted me to arrange the "spiritually impactful" books I had read up to that time on a spreadsheet in the order that I read them. Remarkably, these books were a proxy for my spiritual journey, starting with *Mere Christianity* and progressing through the classic Christian mystics. The list is now up to more than 250 books. I quite literally see these authors as members of the "communion of saints," companions and fellow travelers who help us along the Way.

Friendships can also grow out of our work. One of the great joys of our professional lives is accomplishing significant things with people we enjoy and respect.

Early in my career, I worked with a fellow member of the C-suite who believed in a strong separation between our personal lives and our professional lives. Was he right?

I have concluded that he was not. While friendship should never cloud our business judgment, and sometimes we may have to fire underperforming coworkers who have become friends along the way, I have come to see these relationships at work differently. Strong relationships, grounded in well-founded trust, make for better decision-making and faster execution. Relationships reduce micro-management as people are freed to do what they need to do.

Through the many transactions, commercial contracts, and public company filings we inevitably labor through together, I've developed strong relationships with the general counsels at the companies I've served. When two of us were asked to speak at a conference of aspiring general counsels about the power of a collaborative working relationship between the general counsel and the CFO, we were glad to do it. She and I could speak credibly about how a professional relationship grounded in the mutual trust of one another's competency led to the rapid and successful completion of numerous financial transactions totaling billions of dollars. Besides, our friendship simply made our work time more fun for both of us.

Seeing relationships as ends in themselves has added to my gratitude for the companions God brings alongside us. "Pity anyone who falls and has no one to help them up" (Ecclesiastes 4:10). We do not travel alone. The circuitous but progressive journey of transformation is so much richer and more meaningful when we have the privilege of sharing it with the community of saints, even as we are all in the process of becoming.

Relationships aren't just a part of the journey. The destination of our journey is into ever-deeper relationships with God and our fellow travelers.

FOR REFLECTION

- Think of the many people who have come into your life at different times. How have they helped you along the journey? How might you have helped them?

- Do you feel like you've chosen your traveling companions, or has God chosen them for you?

- Can you see God growing into your most important traveling companion?

PART 3

REALIGNED

BRINGING MEANING
TO OUR WORK

*God makes everything new, including us. Through
his transforming process, we are set free from the
ways we have visibly or invisibly been held back.
Our careers are realigned from self-centered
motivations to God-centered motivations, so our
work becomes an authentic expression of who
God is making us to be.*

19

PURPOSE IN LIFE

AND WORK

Seek first his kingdom and his righteousness,
and all these things will be given to you as well.

MATTHEW 6:33

> **Before we can find meaning in our work, we**
> **have to understand our purpose in life.**

The admissions department of my business school wisely agreed my education would be more valuable if I had some work experience prior to starting the MBA program, so they granted me a deferred admission. Instead of moving from college directly to the graduate program, I first got a job in my home state of Idaho.

But after a year had passed, I was feeling dissatisfied in my work. *Maybe I shouldn't be spending the time before business school working for a corporation*, I thought. *Maybe I should do something that would enhance my compassion for people.*

I went to visit my brother who was attending graduate school in Colorado to evaluate a range of options. I considered working in a soup kitchen and participating in a ministry visiting people in jail. I even thought about living on the street. Our family wasn't wealthy, but I'd never really gone without, at least not for an extended period of time. But none of the alternatives seemed quite right.

Returning home to Idaho from that trip, I concluded that my challenge was not to learn compassion in the isolated experience of a year but to live it out in my daily life. In short, to live an integrated life.

On the heels of that conclusion, I wrote the first entry in the journal that now has reached over ten thousand pages: "I want deeply to get closer to God and to include him in my decisions and my life."

Seven years passed. I earned my MBA. My career was progressing well. But in parallel, the anguish I felt from a lack of meaning in my work had also grown. As I wrestled with this question, I stopped going to church, because I no longer knew if I believed in God. I thought it was hypocritical to worship a God I wasn't sure existed.

In the midst of this wrestling, I reread the opening page of my journal written those seven years previously. The "Aha!" from this rereading would change the trajectory of my life. I'd had it backward all these years: I was trying to fit God into my plans instead of being willing to submit myself to his plan. Even worse was the insidious pride laced through my stated desire. Wasn't it big of me to include the Creator of the universe in my decisions and my life!

Perspective matters.

Ten days after seeing the fallacy of my thinking, I surrendered, responding to Jesus' call to give up everything I have to become his disciple.

Our view of life shapes our view of work, and we will never find meaning in our work until we properly understand the source of purpose in our life. I had to first choose to live for God so he could infuse my work with the meaning only he can provide.

God desires to redeem and restore *all* of creation, including the broken systems and institutions of our work. And he invites us to participate with him in his restoration of our little corner of the world through the activity of work he planned for us long ago.

God had to reframe my perspective of who is God and who is not, of who is the Creator and who is the creation. Though a new creation is born when we surrender to God, this spiritual embryo must grow immeasurably before it approaches maturity.

Even after coming to this understanding, my strong will continued to battle God's. I wasn't living into the truth he was asking of me—to "seek first his kingdom and his righteousness," believing "all these things" (including meaning in work) would be given to me as well. I was fighting God's commands, refusing to allow him to fulfill his purposes in me and for me. It was as though he were saying to this young sapling, "Grow up and be a strong oak tree," and I was saying, "But I'd rather be a yellow pine, or a bear, or a bobcat."

We may not always see or understand God's purpose or plans, but he always has our best interests at heart. Certainly his plans are so much better and grander than our own, for he "is able to do immeasurably more than all we ask or imagine" (Ephesians 3:20). As we shift our focus to the priorities God has for us, our plans for a picnic of bologna sandwiches on the concrete patio in our fenced-in yard will be replaced by his plans for a feast served on a mountain with magnificent views.

> On this mountain the LORD Almighty will prepare
> a feast of rich food for all peoples,
> a banquet of aged wine—
> the best of meats and the finest of wines. (Isaiah 25:6)

Every moment of our lives conspires to bring us into the expansiveness and richness of this life he promises. Every moment contains everything we need to fulfill our deepest purpose in life. The interaction between these exterior and interior worlds stimulates our growth and leads to living the bountiful, seamless life God promises each of us.

So we are left with a choice: either we can choose to live within the designs of the Enemy we carry with us from the fall, or we can choose to live into God's unfolding design for his creatures. God spoke all of creation into being and is still speaking to us today about his design for our lives.

FOR REFLECTION

- In what areas of your life might you be trying to fit God into your plans rather than submitting yourself to God's plans? What's behind that way of thinking?

20

THE THREE KEYS
TO UNHAPPINESS

Do nothing out of selfish ambition or vain conceit.

PHILIPPIANS 2:3

If the Son sets you free, you will be free indeed.

JOHN 8:36

> *Jesus' love releases us from the invisible*
> *prisons of our own making.*

Before our surrender and transformation, we are all stuck. The barriers might be invisible, but they are real. We don't think we are controlled by anyone—yet Jesus has come to set captives free of things we don't even know plague us. Why would Jesus ask us to give up everything we have? He wants to detach us from the things of this world so that we might be free to attach ourselves to God alone.

These prisons are located throughout the land within us and the bars are constructed of a variety of materials. But two I've observed to be nearly universal among businesspeople are achievement and competitiveness. Many of us are wired for achievement to begin with, and then we are thrust into a milieu systematically designed to foster competition. Books, including many bestsellers, have been written on building sustainable competitive advantage.

In the silence of solitude, God reveals the invisible fears and misplaced motives propelling me, and he then goes about his work of freeing me from them. Achievement and competitiveness have been near the top of his rework list for me. He emptied the backpack filled with the burden of potential that had weighed me down since the first time I received straight As in school and my teacher told me that I would go far. He unearthed a deep and devastating desire to become famous for doing good. He revealed just how important I thought it was for me to please others, how I had spent my life doing it and had become good at it.

I lapped up the accolades. I listened for the applause. What I didn't see was the danger I had subjected myself to through years of performing for an audience of more than one.

It would take me years to see that I was living in accordance with what I've come to call the three keys to unhappiness: expecting, comparing, and competing. The sequence goes something like this: set high standards; compare myself with others to see how I'm doing; and compete with others as if we're in an Olympic trial. Without fail, following this prescription will achieve its predictable consequences—self-absorbed disappointment and unhappiness.

The world of business, with its drive for achievement, uncountable metrics comparing actuals to plans, and an inherent structure built on competition, injects these three keys to unhappiness with steroids. One well-accomplished graduate student, about to start a high-powered consulting job, lamented to a group of us in a late-night conversation, "I think my entire educational experience is designed to set me up for unhappiness." He went on to describe how our expectations are elevated by the people around us and by almost every article in the alumni magazine. We are trained to focus on what's left to do rather than celebrating what we've just accomplished, and there will always be someone better, smarter, or richer than we are.

There is no simple solution to operating in the innately and intensively competitive world of business. But there are things we can do. For instance, if we're wired to run as if we're in an Olympic trial, we can focus on our PR rather than a WR—our personal record rather than a world record. The shift from winning to excellence, from competing with others to being the best I can be, can be liberating.

The best antidote to being sucked into the quagmire of competitiveness is to stay close to God. His focus on excellence is exemplary: "God saw all that he had made, and it was very good" (Genesis 1:31). Yet there is no trace of selfish ambition or competitiveness in our all-powerful God. Neither did Jesus cut down others in order to elevate himself. Rather, he emptied himself in order to do the will of the Father, becoming our model.

Jesus wants to open the doors to the prisons we create for ourselves, including those we've locked ourselves into using the three keys to unhappiness.

The contrast between living in the misery imposed by this world and the freedom found in God is striking. I know because I have lived in both. I have lived in the dank, oppressive atmosphere of my own making. And over time I began taking some halting steps from there onto the soft, green grass outside. I have kicked my heels in the air, like a calf running out of the barn onto the green grass of springtime on the ranch where I grew up. There is nothing like the freedom found in God.

This taste of freedom leads to profound gratitude. Every breath becomes a gift from the one who breathed into our nostrils and made us living beings. Thanksgiving pours out of us for the one who has sustained life through the generations and into this very moment.

Nestled in the love of our Father, we are free indeed.

FOR REFLECTION

- Imagine yourself in a prison that is invisible to you. What is it made of? Who put it there?

- And now imagine Jesus opening the door and beckoning you to come out. Do you come? What might be holding you back?

- Imagine yourself stepping across the threshold. Can you experience a sliver of the freedom he is calling you into? What would it take to have this grow into the fullness of freedom he promises?

- How does living in God's freedom influence the way you work in the innately competitive world of business?

21

IDENTITY OR EXPRESSION?

See what great love the Father has lavished on us,
that we should be called children of God!
And that is what we are!

1 JOHN 3:1

> **I am not what I do. Rather, what I do is an**
> **expression of who I am.**

When I was in my midthirties, my continuing anguish over my inability to find meaning in my work impelled me to enroll in a class on faith in the marketplace offered by a Seattle theological school. The first insight came at the beginning of the first class as the fifteen or so participants were introducing ourselves.

The person to the leader's left started, and we went around the circle. When it came to my turn, I responded like most of the others.

"Good morning. My name is Barry Rowan. I am the CFO of Fluke Corporation."

The pattern continued from chair to chair, until one person responded differently.

"My name is Steve. I am a dad and a follower of Christ."

So am I, I thought to myself. *But that wasn't how I identified myself.*

Looking back, I realize it probably wasn't even how I thought of myself.

The myth? We are what we do. The truth? What we do is an expression of who we are.

It is easy, and common, among those of us who are deeply committed to our work to let it take up an oversized position in defining who we are. This distortion in the source of our identity haunts many of us, and it's further compounded for people in positions of leadership.

A CEO friend of mine came home from work one evening and started issuing commands to his wife and children as he was used to doing at the office. His loving but strong wife took him by the hand and led him back out the front door. Pointing to the floor underneath the front door, she said, "When you cross the threshold of our home, you are no longer CEO." And then she reminded him to take the trash out, because Tuesday was garbage day.

I have struggled much to clarify my own identity. If I am not what I do, who am I? Yes, I am Linda's husband and Mark and David's dad, but these are roles I play. Deeper within me, who am I? What does the great I AM have to say about who I am?

The apostle John reveals our true identity in the prologue of his Gospel. "To all who did receive him, to those who believed in his name, he gave the right to become children of God—children born not of natural descent, nor of human decision or a husband's will, but born of God" (John 1:12-13). We are children of the living God!

Are we living like that? All of the time? Some of the time? On the job? As we more properly view our lives from the inside out, we see that our work lives provide an outlet for so much of who we are—our talents, our values, our passions, our energy.

In his book *On Becoming a Leader,* Warren Bennis presents a fascinating definition of leadership: "Leaders are people who are able to express themselves fully." It's not that others can't also express themselves, but this idea of leadership intrigued me. This concept would become foundational to a primary hope I have for my life and for others—to grow into the full expression of ourselves. I know this can become true, because I've seen it in others.

I once attended an event where Bob Farrell, founder of Farrell's Ice Cream Parlours, was the speaker. He described a day at the cash register when he got the whole restaurant to sing "Happy Birthday" to a boy who had been forgotten. As he described the smile on the boy's face, there were tears in his eyes and those of everyone in the audience.

We were all touched by the tender story, but I was moved even more by the example of a man who had found himself in his work. As he made clear in his talk, his life wasn't about ice cream; it was about how his work provided an opportunity to share the love of Jesus. His joy in telling the story said much about a job that allowed for the full expression of the man called to this work.

Our identity lies in God, not in the artificial identities peddled by the world. We are children of God, made in his image. We are his beloved. And when we truly know this about ourselves, we can grow into and live out of that inspirational identity.

FOR REFLECTION

- We have all lived under false identities at one time or another in our lives. Imagine climbing into a time-travel helicopter that takes you back to your high school years and then passes over the phases of your life since then. What are some of the false identities that have defined you across the course of your life?

- And now focus on one of these remembrances. Is there anything you might have done or felt differently if you'd truly lived out of a belief that you are a child of the living God?

- How might you live or lead from where you are now, knowing your identity is as a beloved daughter or son of God?

22

JOB SHARING WITH JESUS

Christic in you, the hope of glory.

COLOSSIANS 1:27

> **All the good we do is an expression
> of Christ in us.**

As Jesus progressively realigns our hearts with the desires of God, our perspective of life is inverted. No longer do we strive to fill ourselves with the right job that will bring us meaning, the right spouse who can make us whole, extreme kayaking trips that will fill us with the rush of adrenaline. No, we are filled with the Spirit of God, and his grace is sufficient for us. And as God fills our deepest parts, the outer extremities of our lives will also be filled with the fullness of life he promises.

This truth of "Christ in us," as Colossians 1:27 says, has profound implications for our daily lives. All the good we do in every action we take becomes an expression of Christ in us. Our work is an expression of the Spirit of God flowing through our unique spiritual DNA into whatever place we find ourselves. What matters is that we, and therefore he, are fully present in the place he has asked us to be.

If Christ is in us, and work is an opportunity for the expression of ourselves, isn't work an opportunity for the expression of the person of Jesus Christ in us?

I accepted the position as CFO of a troubled public company with $900 million in revenue, to see if these perspectives could stand up to the intensity of a turnaround. The company's stock price had skidded from $17 per share at its IPO to less than a dollar, we were losing $50 million a year, and we had over $200 million in debt at 16–20 percent interest rates. One of my first tasks was to renegotiate the debt to, in Linda's words, "break the bondage of the bondholders."

Soon I found myself in the offices of a high-priced New York law firm, taking part in a series of tense, high-stakes negotiations with the hedge fund who owned the debt. These investors were difficult, to say the least. In fact, one of our board members said to me, "Barry, you just have to take as a starting point that these people have no soul." Though this comment may have run counter to my personal theology, I quickly discovered their intensity as we went through ten rounds of negotiations, with the hedge fund's lawyers repeatedly rescinding terms they'd previously offered in order to maximize their financial gain.

Midway through these negotiations, I had a private conversation with our general counsel. He said, "Barry, how is it that you are able to stay calm in the midst of these extraordinarily difficult negotiations?"

Our general counsel was a Jewish man whom I respected deeply. Pulling my tattered travel Bible from my briefcase, I said, "I hope at least some of these words make it from the pages of this book into the pages of my heart. In fact, my perspective is grounded in the Scripture of your own Jewish tradition."

I began reading aloud Psalm 73, which starts with the psalmist upset by the prosperity of the wicked—just as our team was upset with the greed and aggressiveness of our investors. But the psalm pivots in verses 16 and 17:

When I tried to understand all this,
> it troubled me deeply
till I entered the sanctuary of God;
> then I understood their final destiny.

I said to my colleague who would become a friend, "The source of my calm is having an eternal perspective of this temporal situation. One day we will all stand buck naked in front of God. We will be held responsible for what we have done. This applies to me as well as to these badly behaving investors. My job is to devote all my strength to doing what I believe is right in the sight of God, and leave the judgment to him. God's sovereignty is the source of my calm in the midst of these intense negotiations."

And it's not just in high-stakes situations that we have the opportunity to live into what Christ would have us do. Wouldn't Christ in me work with the capable manager on my team to find a creative way for her to work part time so she can spend more time with her struggling teenager? Wouldn't Christ in me detour from a packed executive schedule to pause to talk to the assistant whose friend was in a motorcycle accident over the weekend? Wouldn't Christ in me speak the truth in love to an employee who thought more highly of himself than his work merited?

All we do is made sacred by our Lord's presence. Whatever our hand finds to do, we do it as though working unto him, for that is exactly what we are doing. In fact, it is him doing his work through us. He in us is going to the cleaners to pick up the laundry. He is participating in a meeting to set the budget for next year. Christ in me is hugging our daughter who skinned her knee on the playground.

As God leads us through the process of "self-naughting" (becoming nothing), as the mystics call it, there will be less of us to impede the flow of Christ's Spirit within us and through us. There will be less of us left to be bruised and battered by the harshness of this world. And it will be he who carries our burdens for us. I long to proclaim with Paul the goal of our faith: "I no longer live, but Christ lives in me" (Galatians 2:20)!

FOR REFLECTION

- Where are you on the progression of being no longer you who are living but Christ living in you? To what degree do you feel you have died to your own desires, self-promotion, or self-preservation?

- What does it feel like when Christ is expressing his life through you? Do things happen that seem to be beyond your own capabilities? Do you utter words that somehow don't seem like your own? Do you feel in the flow of the Spirit, part of something much larger than yourself?

- Would it be fun to live more of your life like this? What would it take to do this?

23

 **HIGH EYES**

Set your minds on things above,
not on earthly things.

COLOSSIANS 3:2

Let us run with perseverance the race
marked out for us, fixing our eyes on Jesus,
the pioneer and perfecter of faith.

HEBREWS 12:1-2

> *Fixing our eyes on Jesus elevates our*
> *perspective, and our worldly problems*
> *pale in the light of eternity.*

During a period when it was hot in the kitchen of the executive suite, I lamented to my spiritual director, "I am suffering poorly." I was mired in the mud. My knowledge of the eternal was doing little to tame the torments of the temporal. Instead of radiating the transcendence over suffering demonstrated by the more advanced saints, I was bitter and impatient. I was feeling stuck. My suffering looked nothing like that of the apostles who, after being flogged, "left the Sanhedrin, rejoicing because they had been counted worthy of suffering disgrace for the Name" (Acts 5:41).

My spiritual director pointed me to the letters of Abbot John Chapman, where I came across one letter written to a friend in 1914 that could have been addressed to me:

> We *must* have our times of desolation and trial. How can we show our love of God except by enduring? He showed His love for us by suffering.
>
> Besides, it is such trials that make us humble—we begin to see there is no good in us, no devotion, no stability in good. That must make us see that God is everything.
>
> The way to union with God is by humbling ourselves, by seeing that we have no goodness; and how can we realize this except by being dry and unable to pray or to be self-satisfied?

Through the abbot's words, I realized it was important for me to recognize and admit that I was suffering poorly. The challenges expose the reality that I am not the person I wish I were. They reveal the boundaries of my strength and character and how far I fall short of the glory of God, as I cannot claim with Paul that "I have learned to be content whatever the circumstances" (Philippians 4:11).

Of course, Jesus understands all this. When the rich ruler addresses him as "good teacher," Jesus responds by saying, "Why do you call me good? No one is good—except God alone" (Luke 18:19). Embracing suffering brings us into a humility that recognizes that all of our goodness comes from God. Indeed, the recognition of our "ungoodness" is the beginning of true goodness.

Gratefully, God does make progress in us over time. Little by little, his change is wrought in us. I've seen it in the fifteen years since I lamented of my suffering poorly to my former spiritual director. Since then I have suffered through the challenges of two successful turnarounds, one business failure, and my dear wife being plagued by health issues for ten years.

My current spiritual director asked me during one of our meetings in the midst of these challenges, "Are you grateful?"

I said that I was. My answer surprised me, for gratitude has not come naturally for me. In spite of my hope to not live in accordance with the three keys to unhappiness, I had succumbed to their lure, and the growth of my gratitude was certainly deferred as a result.

I then asked this wise director, a dozen years my senior, why he asked. He said he'd observed, particularly through conversations with the elderly, that everyone's life is characterized both by good times and by challenges, and that people become either bitter or grateful over time.

With full knowledge of the perils of the world, Christ said, "I am sending you out like sheep among wolves. Therefore be as shrewd as snakes and as innocent as doves" (Matthew 10:16). The path between shrewdness and innocence narrows in places to a one-foot-wide traverse along a canyon wall above a rushing river a thousand feet below. It is easy for us sheep to lose our footing, and we all will at times. Our shrewdness may become manipulative, or our innocence may get us slaughtered, but this is not a reason to abandon the Way.

Even as we take the threats in life seriously, it matters where we fix our eyes.

The meekness of surrender draws our eyes to higher heights. "Since, then, you have been raised with Christ, set your hearts on things above, where Christ is, seated at the right hand of God. Set your minds on things above, not on earthly things. For you died, and your life is now hidden with Christ in God" (Colossians 3:1-3).

"High eyes." That was the admonition from our instructor at the racetrack where I learned to drive a car up to 140 miles per hour on a snaking track during one of our father-son adventures. The instructor said, "Keep your eyes up so you can see what's happening in front of you. Where you've been doesn't matter, where you are will be finished in an instant, and where you are going will appear before you know it."

The author of the letter to the Hebrews similarly guided us to have "high eyes," saying, "Let us run with perseverance the race marked out for us, fixing our eyes on Jesus, the pioneer and perfecter of faith. For the joy set before him he endured the cross, scorning its shame, and sat down at the right hand of the throne of God. Consider him who endured such opposition from sinners, so that you will not grow weary and lose heart" (Hebrews 12:1-3).

In the words of Marcel Proust, "The only true voyage of discovery . . . would be not to visit strange lands but to possess other eyes."

We can focus on what is bad in this world, or we can ignore it at our peril. But raising our eyes to the things above—not in spite of pain but in the midst of it—helps to put our temporary predicament into proper perspective.

Suffering is not the end of the story.

FOR REFLECTION

- Recall a time when you were in the midst of suffering. Perhaps it was years ago, a week ago, or even yesterday. Where did you fix your eyes? Would your experience have been changed by having "high eyes"—by fixing your eyes on Jesus?

- Jesus tells us, "The one who endures to the end will be saved" (Matthew 24:13 NLT). How might this perspective change the way you endure and emerge from the troubles of this world?

24

 # SEAMLESSNESS

*All authority in heaven and on earth
has been given to me.*

MATTHEW 28:18

> *The sacred/secular divide is an artificial
> distortion devised by humans. The truth is,
> everything is under the lordship of Christ.*

Early in my career, I read an article about a company revered as one of the world's better-managed businesses. The company was promoting what it called "boundaryless behavior" in an effort to get its hundreds of thousands of employees working as a single organism.

It struck me that I should live a boundaryless life in terms of my faith and work. All I would do, I would do for God. There would be no distinction between my Sunday life and my Monday life. I longed to be in God's will whether I was at home, in the office, or hiking among the Douglas firs of the Pacific Northwest.

The English author Os Guinness helped me, through his book *The Call*, to better understand the false dichotomies underlying my earlier thinking. Guinness described what he called the Protestant distortion and the Catholic distortion. Since I was going to a Protestant church on Sunday and a Catholic church during the week, I figured I had better pay attention—I was probably doubly distorted!

Protestants, in Guinness's view, are more likely to create an artificial distinction between the sacred and the secular. Their distortion is to view some jobs as intrinsically holier than others—being a minister is holier than being a plumber, being a social worker is holier than being a data entry clerk, and so on.

Catholics have a distortion of their own between what they consider to be higher and lower callings. Priests, nuns, and members of religious orders are above the common laity. It is interesting that virtually all of the named saints rise from the ranks of the religious.

Both of these distortions run counter to the truth described in Scripture that everything is under the lordship of Christ. Guinness said, "If all that a believer does grows out of faith and is done for the glory of God, then all dualistic distinctions are demolished."

As God erases these kinds of false dichotomies from our minds, it opens the field of options for finding meaning in the daily work of business. Short of our being in the business of pornography or the manufacture of chemical weapons, it seems virtually anything we do can be done in a way that glorifies God. Few career choices are inherently counter to his call.

My next-order response to this demolished dualism was to seek the connection between what I am doing in this moment and my purpose in life. How does my work life become an extension of my spiritual life? How do the two work together rather than against each other?

One flows from the other in a current of congruence.

When we're trying to decide what to do for the Lord, it isn't always a matter of right or wrong, or higher or lower, but often simply a matter of speaking Jesus' question to Bartimaeus back to our Lord: "What do you want me to do for you?" (Mark 10:51).

FOR REFLECTION

- Viewing everything under the lordship of Christ, how might your daily work bring glory to God?
- Can you articulate a connection between your daily and the divine?

25

LIVING RIGHT HERE, RIGHT NOW

*Be very careful . . . how you live—not as unwise
but as wise, making the most of every opportunity.*

EPHESIANS 5:15-16

*You do not even know what will happen tomorrow.
What is your life? You are a mist that appears for
a little while and then vanishes.*

JAMES 4:14

> **The fullness of life is found by living fully
> in the present moment.**

A remarkable thing happens when, as new creations, we begin to live our life not for ourselves but for God: Every moment becomes a sacrament. We begin to see that each moment contains everything we need to fulfill our deepest purpose in life—to love God with all our heart, mind, soul, and strength, and to love our neighbor as ourselves. We become present to God's presence in the present moment.

Our attitude changes from one of dejection, as we slump in our seats wishing we were somewhere else, to one of gratitude for being in the place where we are. We see that we are where God wants us to be, because if God wanted us to be in a different place, we would be. Catherine of Siena described it this way: "To the true servant of God every place is the right place and every time is the right time."

Some time ago, I was sitting at a table in the dining room of a guest ranch in Colorado during a men's retreat. The wise owner of the ranch said to us, "Wherever you are, be all there." His words stuck with me and often come back to me, particularly when I find myself in places *besides* where I am.

Similarly, one of my friends is fond of saying to us goal-oriented types, "Next steals now."

Living fully in the present moment has been one of the most important and yet most difficult concepts of the spiritual life for me to live. The overachiever of my youth still has a voice within me, steering me to focus on what's left to accomplish in the future rather than living in gratitude for the present. The thief who would have next steal now still prowls around my house seeking to rob me of the joy of living in the only place we find true life.

We can and should remember the past and plan for the future, but that's not where we find life. We can only live right here, right now.

Perhaps this is why God describes himself as the great "I AM" (Exodus 3:14). He is the eternal present. We can only meet him where we are and as we are.

This lesson was brought home to me during a difficult refinancing we were doing for a company I was brought in to help turn around. We were in the process of raising $200 million to pay off the company's usurious debt. The commitments were due on a Tuesday, and we'd received $90 million in new commitments by the night before.

I was sitting in church after Mass that Tuesday morning. By the end of the day, we would either pop the champagne corks, celebrating a successful refinancing, or we would have to pull ourselves up by our bootstraps and slog through whatever difficult next steps would be required to pay off our bondholders. As I wrestled with these two very different outcomes that could occur by the end of the day, I sensed God saying to me, "Are you willing to embrace my will that is embedded in your circumstances?" After another thirty minutes of wrestling with the question—strongly preferring the champagne over the muck boots—I finally said, "Yes, Lord. I will do your will."

Oswald Chambers bid us, "Arise and do the next thing." Our work is to do what the present moment asks of us. It might be making calls in an effort to find that next job, accepting that I have to redirect my efforts when a major project gets derailed, or remaining alert in a meeting to help advance the discussion. It might be taking the first step across the crevasse of an icy relationship, going for a walk to clear my head, taking time to pray, or savoring a great meal with gratitude for the gift of taste and the friends who are enjoying it together.

How do we know what to do? We go to God. A posture of spiritual surrender seeks God's will for our lives in each moment. As moments pile on moments to become lifetimes, we find ourselves in an uninterrupted conversation with God.

Each moment of this lifelong joint adventure of walking daily in the divine prompts us to ask, "Is there something I should say now? God, what is your will for me right here, right now? What are you teaching me in this moment?" As we develop the spiritual eyes to see, we'll increasingly see God's will and his word embedded in every moment.

Perhaps we will then ask fewer questions of God and pay more attention to the questions he asks of us. "How are you experiencing my love? Will you empty yourself of your own desires so that I might pour myself into this person or this situation right now? Will you drop your nets to come and see?"

All we are goes wherever we go. And our entire lives are preparation for the present moment we find ourselves in. Our call is to bring all of who we are to every moment of our lives. I was once asked to speak to a group of people over lunch at a Seattle corporate office. I admitted to my host as I entered the boardroom that in the crush of my schedule, I hadn't found time to prepare any notes. I quipped, "We'll consider that all of my life has been preparation for this moment," and I proceeded to share what was on my heart.

Saint Bonaventure said, "The heart is free that is held by no love other than the love of God." Being present in the present is to be who God asks us to be, to do what he asks us to do—right here, right now.

FOR REFLECTION

- Write down three to five activities you might go through on a typical day. For each activity, jot down a thought about what it might look like for you to engage in that activity, first according to your own will, and then according to God's will.

- What emotions does this exercise elicit for you?

26

ALIGNMENT WITH GOD

Do not conform to the pattern of this world,
but be transformed by the renewing of your mind.
Then you will be able to test and approve what
God's will is—his good, pleasing and perfect will.

ROMANS 12:2

> *Our lives and our work become meaningful*
> *as our heart and actions are aligned with*
> *the divine design.*

After working flat-out for twenty-five years, I took a "purposeful pause" in my career when I turned fifty. I was deeply fatigued and longed for a break. Our company had just been sold and I had some financial flexibility, so I decided not to immediately seek another full-time executive role.

In music, the rests are what give it richness. Linda's and my theme during this time was "Don't slur the rest."

I began praying for one to two hours a day. I started going to daily Mass after a friend told me, "There's a cumulative effect to receiving Communion every day for at least a month." (He was right.) A year into the purposeful pause, I found the courage to embark on my first eight-day silent retreat, and these extended periods away would become a nearly annual tradition.

I spent my second silent retreat at a place perched on a cliff above the shores of Puget Sound. One night, unable to sleep, I climbed out of my bed and walked down the 180 steps to the beach below. The moon lit the steps and created a glorious reflection off the water that dissolved into the dark pines lining the bank beside me. As I stepped onto the beach, the crunch of the pebbles pressing into the sand and the delicate lapping of the waves were the only whispers breathed into the still, moonlit night.

Then, in a sudden shift, the moment was magnified as I saw the beauty infused with power. I was overcome by the hydrology of Puget Sound. *The changing tides must move trillions of gallons of water in and out of the channels within this intricate shoreline every day,* I thought.

This realization released a flood of tender tears, as I realized God was speaking his truth to me through the physical world. Scripture tells us, after all, that God "gave the sea its boundary" (Proverbs 8:29). Overwhelmed by the genius of God's design and its elegance in execution, I thought, *Wouldn't I rather live within the divine design than outside of it?*

We are purposeful beings, and we want to live our lives on purpose. As we scurry about doing our work, how do we know that these hours are not wasted, that they are lived within the divine design? How can we see that they fulfill our deepest purpose and highest calling?

A Jewish religious expert once asked Jesus to name the greatest commandment. Jesus did him better by naming two. " 'Love the Lord your God with all your heart and with all your soul and with all your mind.' This is the first and greatest commandment. And the second is like it: 'Love your neighbor as yourself.' All the Law and the Prophets hang on these two commandments" (Matthew 22:37-40).

To love God and to love our neighbors—this sums up our chief aim and purpose in life. It also provides a practical way of knowing whether we are living our lives on purpose or not. The test for us at every moment of life is to ask, Is what I am doing expressing love of God or love of people?

My purposeful pause was a restorative time. It also dramatically deepened my relationship and intimacy with God. But after two and a half years, Linda and I came to a shared and mutually surprising decision over dinner en route to visit our older son in college. We concluded I should go back to a full-time executive job. My energy had been rekindled, and we both felt strongly about the power of business to contribute to a better society. I also wanted to take a job that would test whether the principles in this book would stand up to the heat of the kitchen.

I decided to join a company requiring a comprehensive turn-around—financially, operationally, strategically, and reputationally. Gratefully, the ideas not only held up but were further refined by the enormous challenges I stepped into.

Living in congruence with the divine design is central to the whole of our lives, but it is particularly relevant to our work lives. The test of this congruence is whether we can explicitly connect our actions in this moment with God's purpose for our life. Given that our whole life is the summation of the moments of our lives, making this connection in each moment means we will live a life on purpose.

Like the confluence of two streams, our spiritual lives and our work lives converge in the moments of our days—sitting in the leather chairs around the boardroom table debating next year's budget, sitting across the table from an employee doing a performance review, flying overseas to meet with distribution channel partners. God's Spirit is in us, animating us, in each of these situations.

While our rebellious nature may fight against it, our true nature seeks to live in surrender to God's design. And as we do, divine joy will flow more freely within us and through us.

FOR REFLECTION

- As you think about your own life and your career, are there times when you felt that you were living in congruence with the divine design? How about in divergence from it? How would you describe the difference in feelings you experienced during these contrasting times?

- Can you see how the streams of your work and your spirituality might come together? Are there ways you might be able to live more fully in the confluence of these two streams of your life?

27

LOVE YOUR WORK

Whatever you do, work at it with all your heart,
as working for the Lord.

COLOSSIANS 3:23

> *Our perspective of work can be life giving*
> *or life draining. God's perspective brings*
> *meaning to our work.*

How we conceive of our work has much to do with how, and how well, we perform our work. If I am working on computer spreadsheets all day, I might be wearied by seeing my job as writing formulas to populate hundreds of electronic cells. But if I see these calculations as a means of developing an annual budget that contributes to the success of a company that makes an important contribution to the common good, won't my work have more meaning than being a spreadsheet monkey?

And so it is with virtually any role. We can bring a life-giving or a life-draining perspective to any job. One inspires us; the other tires us.

In fact, it seems that one validation of whether we are called to a role by God is whether we can genuinely bring a life-giving perspective to the work. As John Eldredge says in his book *Wild at Heart*, "Don't start by asking what the world needs. Start by asking what makes me come alive, for what the world needs are people who are alive!"

I love kids, but I would be drained by being around six-year-olds all day every day. A gifted first-grade teacher, called to this work, would be energized by the opportunity to give these children the gift of learning.

My dad practiced as a veterinarian in Idaho for over seventy years, and even after what his partners called his "fifth annual retirement party," he continued to work until he gave up his license at age ninety-six. He was one of the hardest-working people I have ever known, but sitting at our kitchen table after breakfast one morning, he said to Linda and me, "I haven't worked a day in my life." He loved what he did.

Many days of my life have seemed a lot like work, but the tasks have been made much more meaningful by a line-of-sight connection between my role in the company and the company's role in society. If I can see how my role in the organization connects with the purpose of the organization, and then how the organization has a higher purpose of contributing to society, and, at the highest level, how the institution participates in God's plan for redeeming the world, that is inspiring. It brings meaning to my work. These connections get me out of bed in the morning. Believing I exist to line the already gilded pockets of investors with more gold would leave me languishing under the covers.

As we look at the contrasting perspectives a worker might bring to his or her work, a theme emerges: life-draining perspectives are self-centered, while life-giving perspectives are others-centered. I believe this is because a life-giving perspective provides an outlet for the expression of love. Seeing my work in this way would naturally be life giving, since loving God and neighbor are Jesus' highest commands to us as his followers. And surely living in accordance with God's design is essential to experiencing the fullness of joy Jesus promises.

While we will never love every minute of our work this side of heaven, a life-giving perspective of our work can bring more love into our work. And the more we see our work as love, the more we will love our work.

FOR REFLECTION

- Start by drawing a line down the center of a piece of paper and label the two columns "Life draining" and "Life giving."

- Thinking about your current job, list in the left column those aspects of your job that one might find life draining. On the right side, make a list of life-giving aspects of your job.

- To get you started, here is an example for a hospice worker: A life-draining perspective might be "I change bedpans for a living for people who are going to die anyway." A life-giving perspective might be "I am creating an environment of unconditional love for people in the precious last days of their lives."

- Which column seems to carry more weight for you?

28

FROM DRUDGERY TO GIFT

*That each of them may eat and drink, and find
satisfaction in all their toil—this is the gift of God.*

ECCLESIASTES 3:13

> *Our work is transformed from drudgery to gift
> when viewed through the eyes of God.*

I may have looked like a young corporate executive when I walked
out the door in the morning, dressed in a suit and tie, briefcase in
hand. But on the inside in the early days of my career, I felt more like
I was a construction worker outfitted with a hard hat and steel-toed
boots bracing himself for the daily toil.

My job back then was tough labor as I wrestled to find meaning
in my work. Without God's clarifying perspective of my work, I found
myself walking haltingly down the path of my career, never fully able
to commit. The "joy of work" was not in my vocabulary.

As I continued to seek answers, my perspective of work underwent
a dramatic revolution through immersing myself in Scripture, particularly the books of Genesis and Ecclesiastes.

Reading the story of Eden, we find this: "The LORD God took the
man and put him in the Garden of Eden to work it and take care of
it" (Genesis 2:15). The fall occurred later, and then God told Adam,

"By the sweat of your brow you will eat your food until you return to the ground" (Genesis 3:19).

The lesson embedded in the sequencing of these verses was a huge "Aha!" for me: God designed work *before* the fall. Work was part of God's original design. Therefore, like all that God made, work is good.

The cursing of work—making it feel like painful drudgery—was not God's original design. His original design was for us to be co-creators with him. And today, even in this fallen, temporary world, he infuses our work with eternal significance.

This grand truth became personal to me through the words of the Preacher in Ecclesiastes. He, too, had moments of disillusionment about work. "What do workers gain from their toil?" he asked; he called work a "burden" (Ecclesiastes 3:9-10). Then he arrived at this answer: "I know that there is nothing better for people than to be happy and to do good while they live. That each of them may eat and drink, and find satisfaction in all their toil—this is the gift of God" (vv. 12-13).

God not only invites us to work alongside him; finding satisfaction in our toil is a gift God wants to give us.

I was only able to tear at a corner of the wrapping paper of this gift, as it would remain in the box for eight years after committing my life to Christ. But knowing God wants people to find satisfaction in *all* their toil inspired me to understand and live into this truth. I prayed for my work to be transformed. I longed for it to go from hard labor wrought by the sweat of my brow to a blessing bestowed by God. Over time God has answered this prayer.

So how does our work go from drudgery to gift? By replacing our misplaced perspective of work with God's perspective of our work.

I hope all of us have many good days when our work excites and satisfies us, when we can see how the work we're doing advances God's purposes on earth. But when we have the other kind of days, we can remember that our toil itself is a gift from God. And may this understanding fill us with hope and inspire us to do our work with excellence, "with all [our] heart, as working for the Lord" (Colossians 3:23).

FOR REFLECTION

- To what degree are you able to "find satisfaction in your toil"? What might you need to do to more fully unwrap this gift from God?

- If you were to see yourself as "working for the Lord," how would that change your attitude? Your work ethic? Your relationships on the job?

29

ASSETS UNDER MANAGEMENT

To the LORD your God belong the heavens,
even the highest heavens, the earth and
everything in it.

DEUTERONOMY 10:14

> **God gives us our work to give back to him.**

For a long time, I looked at my work and its rewards just like most people do—as *mine*.

I may not have said these things, but I thought them: *I* toiled through years of schooling to earn a high-quality education. *I* worked hard, made sacrifices, and took risks to succeed on the job. *My* promotions, *my* salary, and the trajectory of *my* career belonged to *me*.

But as the commitment to live my life for God instead of myself began to send its roots down within me, I progressively understood better what that means for my work life. The profound implication of our decision to live our lives for God is that *nothing is ours*. Nothing! It's not about tithing 10 percent. It's about God owning 100 percent. Every single dimension of our lives belongs to God: our talents, our money, our marriages, our kids. And our careers.

"What do you have that you did not receive?" the apostle Paul asks. "And if you did receive it, why do you boast as though you did not?" (1 Corinthians 4:7).

Over time, I began to see a cycle of giving in relationship with God. He endows us with gifts and talents, which we can choose to give back to him. As we return them to him, he gives them back to us to manage and grow on his behalf. In the same way that we love because he first loved us, we give because he has given to us. We are stewards of what God has given us, so that all we have might be given for the benefit of others.

People who manage money for a living describe the scope of their responsibilities as "AUM"—assets under management. Just as a private wealth manager has assets under management measured in dollars, which of God's assets do we have under management? Perhaps our God-given AUM could be measured in terms of money, but the measures also surely include our talent, our education, our experiences, our relationships, and our character. We are even called to be stewards of our story. How might my story be told for the benefit of others? (Hopefully, these writings are a version of that.)

Under this new paradigm, we discover ourselves to be coworkers with God.

I once heard Rich Stearns, former CEO of World Vision (the largest faith-based relief organization in the world), describe his work in serving those who are impoverished this way: "God may own 'the cattle on a thousand hills,' but somebody has to butcher them and turn them into steaks."

Being a steward of God's assets is a high calling. Every one of us has a genuine and important role to play in what God is doing in the world. But we can make the most of our role only as we remember who is the true Owner of everything. And he expects us, as every owner would, to grow the value of what he has given us to manage. Remember the parable of the talents: the owner rewarded the one who made the most of his talents with even more (Matthew 25:14-30).

Those times when we might be feeling proud or possessive about our work may be an invitation to wrestle with the truth that our work is not our own. Within our spirit, through the work of God's Spirit, perhaps we can begin making the transition from owner to steward.

God has given all of us many assets to manage, including seeming intangibles we might not readily consider. For example, take something somewhat obscure such as the ability to make intuitive decisions based on sound business judgment. Early in my career, I was much more analytical than intuitive; reluctant, even, to rely on an intuition I couldn't yet trust. But through his grace, God gives us gifts and grows these gifts. Through making literally thousands of business decisions over the years, my business judgment has grown significantly. I believe it has now become an asset. Every asset we have been given is for the benefit of God's kingdom.

A major source of the sustaining joy I've more fully experienced in these latter years of my career is through knowing I am stewarding the assets *of and for* the Creator of the universe for the benefit of his creation. I think that's a pretty cool calling.

FOR REFLECTION

- Take stock of the assets God has placed under your care. Make a list of them.

- What would it mean for you to place all of your assets into the hands of God? Can you see him placing them back into your hands as his steward?

- And how might you grow what he has given you, so they might be used for the benefit of others?

30

WHY DO WE WORK?

"My food," said Jesus, *"is to do the will of him who sent me and to finish his work."*

JOHN 4:34

> ### *We don't derive meaning* from *our work.*
> ### *Rather, we bring meaning* to *our work.*

On one of my many business trips—I would end up traveling two million miles on a single airline over twenty-five years—I was on a shuttle bus going from one of the outlying airport parking lots to the terminal. Never one to pass up an opportunity to save a few bucks, I'd chosen the lowest-cost parking lot, and I found myself sitting on this bus with a band of fellow cheapskates.

Most of the previous parking lot buses I'd ridden on were piloted by drivers who had been worn down to a zombie-like state. And who wouldn't be? The driver circles between parking lot and terminal every twenty-six minutes for eight hours a day, every day.

But this driver was different. Looking to be in her late thirties, she was chatting it up with all the passengers. She asked them what they did for work and where they were going, with an easy smile and authentic interest. She practically jumped out of her seat to help the travelers with their luggage. Unmanufactured joy radiated from her.

My stop was the last one, and after everyone else had unloaded from the bus, my curiosity bubbled over.

"Do you like your job?" I asked the driver.

"I *love* my job," was her instantaneous answer. "I meet interesting people going interesting places," she answered crisply. Amazingly, her tone contained not a hint of jealousy toward these people going to these interesting places while she was stuck driving her airport circuit. It wasn't her work that was her source of meaning. It was her perspective of her work.

If we're struggling with a sense of meaning in our work, the real challenge is not finding a job with a high degree of intrinsic meaning; our challenge to find joy apart from our circumstances is in developing a perspective that brings meaning to our work, regardless of the level of meaning intrinsically provided by our job. None of us ever has to cry, "Meaningless! Meaningless!" about our job, like the exasperated Preacher in Ecclesiastes 2:17-26.

Seeing his work as doing the will of the one who sent him was the source of Jesus' very sustenance. As this also becomes true for us, we can embrace the Preacher's eventual conclusion: "Whatever your hand finds to do, do it with all your might" (Ecclesiastes 9:10). And know that we will be nourished by it.

There is no meaning apart from God. Conversely, everything has meaning when done out of love for him. The twentieth-century priest Josemaría Escrivá wrote, "Add a supernatural motive to your ordinary professional work, and you will have sanctified it."

FOR REFLECTION

- Have you ever relied on your job to give your life meaning? Was it successful, or was it ultimately disappointing?

- Being able to articulate a perspective of our work that emanates from our heart brings meaning to the many hours we'll spend working. It might even be evidence of God's calling.

- How can you bring greater meaning *to* your work?

PART 4

SENT

FULFILLING GOD'S WILL IN THE WORLD

As we move into the world in right relationship with God, living for purposes beyond ourselves, we are in a better position to also nudge the world toward right relationship with him. We can release the power of business to contribute to a better society as seen through the eyes of God.

31

SHALOM

[God] has committed to us the message
of reconciliation. We are therefore Christ's
ambassadors, as though God were making
his appeal through us.

2 CORINTHIANS 5:19-20

. . . so that God may be all in all.

1 CORINTHIANS 15:28

> **As God brings us into peace, we will be**
> **channels of his peace into the world.**

Jesus' work on the cross bridges the division between sinful humanity and our holy God. "God was pleased to have all his fullness dwell in him, and through him to reconcile to himself all things, whether things on earth or things in heaven, by making peace through his blood, shed on the cross" (Colossians 1:19-20).

The apostle Paul considered himself, and us, to be ambassadors for this reconciliation. "He has committed to us the message of reconciliation. We are therefore Christ's ambassadors, as though God were making his appeal through us" (2 Corinthians 5:19-20).

What is this reconciliation? It's personal, as we as individuals come to faith in Christ. But it's much bigger than that—it is cosmic.

The Father, who so loved the world and sent his only Son to redeem it, invites us to help bring the world into right relationship with him and with all of his creation.

The Hebrew word *shalom* helps us understand what reconciliation looks like on earth. Shalom is not just "hello" and "goodbye." It conveys the sense of a comprehensive peace, harmony, wholeness, prosperity, and well-being.

A world of shalom is a world where everything is in right relationship with everything else: us with God, us with one another, us with the world. This includes being in right relationship with the work God has called us to do. A wrong relationship with our work might be a reluctant obedience to God's will. A more right relationship with our work might be evidenced by a posture of giving generously of ourselves for the benefit of others out of genuine joy and without compulsion.

Augustine of Hippo spoke about this shalom in his description of the City of God: "The peace of the heavenly City lies in a perfectly ordered and harmonious communion of those who find their joy in God and in one another in God. Peace, in its final sense, is *the calm that comes of order*." There is a proper order to this world, and our peace comes when we live in congruence with God's design.

Our work lives offer us an almost continuous opportunity to nudge the world closer to this godly congruence. This happens when our purposes are aligned with God's purposes, when we see the purpose of business as being an instrument of God's purposes.

At its core, business involves organizing the work of people in ways that enable each of us to maximize our contribution to the mission of the organization. Disorder leads to inefficiency, so perhaps our role as business leaders is to restore a bit of divine orderliness.

One simple description of entrepreneurship that I like is to "find a need and fill it." If businesses are going to be sustainably successful, they must deliver products and services that fulfill genuine human needs in accordance with the way people live, or will live, their lives.

But this idea can be applied to a wide range of professions. Orthopedic surgeons replace knees so grandparents can stay active with their grandchildren. English teachers teach children so they can express themselves more fully through language. Architects design buildings to be congruent with the landscape—the work of God and people dwelling side-by-side.

When we are right with God, we can be right with the world and serve as God's ambassadors, bringing the world into proper relationship with him. Living our lives under the lordship of Christ is the source of our deepest shalom, and this peaceful centeredness can then flow out from us and into the world around us through all we do.

FOR REFLECTION

- Can you recall a situation when you were transformed on the interior by God in some meaningful way and this caused you to act differently on the exterior? Perhaps God dissipated your anger so you were able to bring peace to a situation. Perhaps your mind was disordered and confused, and through prayer came a clarity that enabled you to provide clarity to others.

- Today, where do you see the opposite of shalom before you, giving you the privilege of creating greater wholeness, peace, and well-being?

32

FLUENT IN LOVE

You are the light of the world. A town built on
a hill cannot be hidden. Neither do people
light a lamp and put it under a bowl. Instead
they put it on its stand, and it gives light to
everyone in the house. In the same way,
let your light shine before others, that they
may see your good deeds and glorify your
Father in heaven.

MATTHEW 5:14-16

> *Love spoken through words without action*
> *leaves an echo of hypocrisy. Love spoken*
> *through action can change the world.*

In the spring of 2001, I was sitting in my office in São Paulo, Brazil, at 7:30 in the morning with a heavy heart. We had just laid off fifteen hundred of our four thousand employees to save this large-scale start-up company from bankruptcy. While we'd made every effort to communicate the news with a sense of humanity, providing extensive outplacement services and receiving not a single lawsuit as a result of the layoffs, the pain was still raw.

As I sat in my chair with the sun streaming in through the corner window, our executive assistant, Anna Lima, discreetly approached my door and said in a soft voice, "Barry, could I ask you a question?"

I said, "Of course. What's on your mind?"

She then asked tenderly, "Are you a Christian?"

I was cautious about where this conversation was headed. I didn't know Anna Lima well. I was still a novice in understanding Brazilian culture. And I didn't want to say anything that would seem inappropriate for someone in my professional position. On the other hand, maybe this was a chance to follow Peter's admonition to "always be prepared to give an answer to everyone who asks you to give the reason for the hope that you have" (1 Peter 3:15).

Yet, as these doors to conversation open, particularly in today's pluralistic environment, it can be tricky to know how to act. How should we live as followers of Jesus in a multicultural, multireligious world, where speaking openly about faith at work is increasingly seen not only as inappropriate but as aggression? The story of Pentecost speaks into this dilemma.

During that time, the Holy Spirit filled the disciples, and "a crowd came together in bewilderment, because each one heard their own language being spoken" (Acts 2:6). I used to think of this only as people from Greece hearing Greek, Arabs hearing Arabic, and so on. But we can read these words at a deeper, more personal level.

God speaks to each of us in a language we can understand. The language we hear from him is individually tailored to each of us: Barry-ese, Nicole-ese, John-ese. He speaks to us uniquely through our circumstances, perhaps asking us to forgive a coworker, or liberating us from fear as we prepare to speak in front of a large group. He speaks to us through words spoken by a friend or from a podium as we absorb a truth God has uniquely sensitized us to receive. Scripture, as the living and active Word of God, penetrates each of our hearts in different ways and at different times.

God speaks to us unceasingly in ways designed for us to hear—and he asks us to go and do likewise. My hope is that the language others hear from me is a language of integrity, a commitment to doing what is right, and a willingness to stop in the hall to ask a co-worker how they or their family members are doing. We preach the gospel through the courage to be direct when directness is needed, through shattering a tense moment in a meeting with a bolt of humor, and by keeping a steady hand on the tiller as we guide a company through turbulent waters.

In my encounter with Anna Lima, I hoped my behavior on the job had prepared the way for this conversation.

She had asked me if I were a Christian. And although I more often describe myself as a follower of Jesus rather than as a Christian, particularly in international settings where the word *Christian* carries some heavy baggage, I knew what she meant. I simply responded, "Yes, I am. Why do you ask?"

She said, "I know you have had to do some very hard things since you took over as CEO a few months ago. But you have brought a spirit of calm and a steadiness to our company. You have treated people with dignity and respect even in the midst of the tremendous challenges we've faced, and I just wondered if it was because you are a Christian."

As Anna Lima stepped out of my office, I turned my face from the door and burst into tears.

God's gifts come wrapped in all kinds of packages.

I pray that the language we speak as followers of Jesus operating in the harshness of this world will be a language others understand—that they will each hear love spoken in "their own language."

FOR REFLECTION

■ When have you been spoken to in a language of love you could understand? What was this language? How would you describe the emotions of this experience?

- Can you also recall a time when you have spoken love to someone, particularly when love seemed absent? How did they respond?
- How might God be asking you to express his love in your current circumstances?

33

BEYOND OURSELVES

I can do all this through him who gives me strength.

PHILIPPIANS 4:13

> **God calls us into the place of our strength,
> but into positions beyond our strength.**

We had just spent nearly two years successfully turning Gogo around, coming out of some major issues arising from a new technology deployment, when the world was shut down by the Covid-19 pandemic. As the company that installs internet on airplanes, we found our business plans more than slightly impacted, with airline flight counts down 96 percent the next month.

The six weeks leading up to Easter of that year were what I described as *an unrelenting Lent*. I struggled to muster the energy to embrace the double turnaround demanded by these circumstances.

The transformation of my perspective and accompanying energy would come through meditating on the lives of Moses and Mary. Moses' heart progressed from a cautious reluctance in his conversation with God at the burning bush, telling God to send someone else (Exodus 3), to a softened suppleness later in his life as he was described as "a very humble man, more humble than anyone else on the face of the earth" (Numbers 12:3). Mary's shift, in the short paragraph describing her conversation with the angel Gabriel, seems equally dramatic as she went from asking, "How will this be?" (Luke 1:34) to "May it be done to me according to your word" (v. 38 NASB). I'd long seen her response as an act of selfless humility, but now I also saw it as an act of profound generosity as she gave her entire life to God's purposes.

Through the lives of these models lived centuries ago, God was speaking to me in the present moment. I sensed God asking me to go *from reluctant obedience to joyful generosity*. Was I willing to give generously and completely of myself as Gogo's CFO, doing whatever I could to help save the company and the employees' jobs? I'd seen versions of this movie before, even if the scenes weren't quite as scary as this one. Would I give this my all, even as I was still drained from the first turnaround of the company?

I would work as hard over the next twelve months as I had at any time in my career.

We developed a three-part plan that included identifying sufficient expense cuts to avoid running out of cash (built around sixteen levers, saving $350 million over the next eighteen months), selling the division that was bleeding $100 million per year from its international operations, and then recapitalizing the (hopefully) remaining business, which would be a much better credit story. In the midst of the crisis the outcome was far from certain, and our investors' sentiment reflected this precariousness as our stock lost over 80 percent of its value. Gratefully, the results exceeded even our highest hopes as the company's market value grew from a low of $125 million to over $2 billion in less than two years.

I've seen the same dynamic over and over in my career and in that of other women and men I've known who are surrendered to God. That is, God calls us into the place of our strength but into positions beyond our strength. In situations like these, it really isn't *our* capability that matters, anyway. What matters is what *God* can do through us. Our strength is finite; God's is infinite.

The apostle Paul experienced this kind of I-don't-have-what-it-takes situation repeatedly, and he actually came to welcome it, even to revel in it. Paul was plagued with an acute physical ailment that surely hindered his apostolic travel and church-planting work. He reflected on it this way:

> In order to keep me from becoming conceited, I was given a thorn in my flesh, a messenger of Satan, to torment me. Three times I pleaded with the Lord to take it away from me. But he said to me, "My grace is sufficient for you, for my power is made perfect in weakness." Therefore I will boast all the more gladly about my weaknesses, so that Christ's power may rest on me. That is why, for Christ's sake, I delight in weaknesses, in insults, in hardships, in persecutions, in difficulties. For when I am weak, then I am strong. (2 Corinthians 12:7-10)

Thankfully, I have enjoyed good health most of my life, but the places God has called me in business have often taken me way beyond things I could do in my own strength or capabilities. Each time that has happened, it has increased my reliance on God. The truth of "When I am weak, then I am strong" is increasingly working its way through the dough of my soul.

It's also encouraging to observe that God doesn't usually ask us to do things that are completely disconnected from our gifting. I have no (and I do mean zero) singing talent. You wouldn't call me to be a part of the church choir . . . and, gratefully, neither has God! Within the realm of business—where I do have some talent—God frequently calls me to do things that are way beyond my own strength or capabilities.

It also seems that the size of our challenges corresponds to the depth of God's work in us. As we are pushed beyond ourselves, we are pushed to trust God all the more. We won't get past the insurmountable obstacle, succeed in the hopeless attempt, or reach the unattainable goal unless we trust in the Lord with all our heart instead of leaning on our own understanding. When we do trust, and see that trust crowned with success as seen through the eyes of God (though not necessarily through the eyes of the world), we'll be better equipped to prayerfully approach the next seemingly impossible thing through a posture of surrender.

Nothing will be impossible with God. (Luke 1:37 ESV)

FOR REFLECTION

- What seemingly impossible thing are you currently confronting? Can you give it to God, recognizing that nothing is impossible with him?

- Try repeating this prayer ten times—slowly, meditatively: "Dear Jesus, I've given my life to you, and I give this situation to you. Please do with it as you will."

34

THE SECRET
OF FRUITFULNESS

I am the vine; you are the branches. Whoever
abides in me and I in him, he it is that bears
much fruit, for apart from me you can do nothing.

JOHN 15:5 ESV

> *Though we may be wired for striving, our*
> *greater work will be achieved through abiding.*

One of the more difficult dimensions of the spiritual life is knowing what responsibility belongs to us and what belongs to God. For action-oriented, hard-driving businesspeople fueled by the high octane of achievement, it is hard to learn that our primary role in our relationship with Jesus is to abide.

It was apparently hard for the disciples too, because Jesus was insistent with them about the importance of abiding: "Abide in me, and I will abide in you. Just as the branch cannot produce fruit by itself unless it abides in the vine, neither can you unless you abide in me" (John 15:4 ISV). How much can we do apart from Jesus? He quantifies it for us: "Nothing!" (v. 5).

The truth Jesus is stating is very clear. Yet it's not easy for me to abide. I want to move when he wants me to stay. I want to squirm out of my circumstances when he wants me to learn from them. But gradually, I think I'm beginning to get the point.

Indeed, my prayer has shifted over the years from asking God to change my circumstances to praying to see God's will *in* my circumstances. If God didn't want me to be here, I wouldn't be here, so what does he want me to learn from this difficult relationship? From the pain of this failure? From the perseverance he seeks from me in the midst of this confusion? How might he want to use me to help this situation, perhaps to bring his peace or to clarify a vision so his people might prosper?

Abiding has led me into what I have come to call "immersion prayer." This prayer most often occurs at the confluence of my circumstances and Scripture, immersed in the presence of God. In these times of solitude, God will show me what he has to teach me through my circumstances or how I should respond to them. My role is to abide and to listen. For example, the decision to pivot our renewable fuels start-up into the agricultural business after failing to raise the next round of financing came out of sitting with Jesus in the Garden of Gethsemane and watching him go from anxiety to resolve. The strength to accept that I might have to pull on my boots and restart a $200 million financing if the orders didn't materialize came as I sat in the back of the church pouring myself and my concerns out to God.

Abiding is not passive. Far from it. It means diligently seeking God and his will in every situation. It means immersing myself in Scripture. It means listening as hard as I can. It means adopting a posture of surrender and changing course as the situation demands it.

As I've been recruited to help turn around troubled companies, I've seen a clear parallel between spiritual abiding and being a listening leader.

The temptation is to come in with guns blazing, to take immediate action. After all, the company is usually on the operating table and hemorrhaging cash. But I've learned that superior long-term results are achieved by going slowly initially to go faster later.

I've come to call it *hypothesis leadership*. Before joining the organization, I do my homework to form a point of view about what appear to be the right steps to help the company. I then keep these notes stuffed in my briefcase and spend a lot of time listening to people, asking questions, doing deep dives into the data. I try to listen carefully to test the accuracy of my hypotheses. These initial ideas are inevitably reshaped by the inputs from the team, who almost always know the details of the business much better than I do. I find this immersion to be critical to setting the right course and ensuring alignment and buy-in from the people who will be responsible for executing the plan.

Companies are likely to grow more fully into their potential by their leaders taking an appropriate amount of time—to listen; to implement well-considered, strategic solutions; and to identify and eliminate the toxicities in the soil of a culture that may prevent the roots of change from taking hold.

Similarly, as we abide in God, we give him permission to till the soil of our souls, to plant the seeds of good trees that will bear much fruit. Jesus used seeds and yeast and little children to paint a picture of the kingdom of God. These all need time to grow and develop into what they are intended to become.

Can I also abide in Jesus to allow his Spirit to grow in me? If I do, perhaps I will achieve something more than the nothing I can achieve apart from him.

FOR REFLECTION

- What does striving versus abiding look like for you?
- Are there places in your life where you might benefit from slowing down, taking time to breathe, to pray, to listen? Might

abiding help you gain clarity, deepen your conviction, enable you to live out of a place of peace?

■ Can you feel the love of God wash over you as you give him this space to do his work?

35

HOW MAY I HELP?

*Each of you should use whatever gift you
have received to serve others.*

1 PETER 4:10

> **Though our old self may seek to be served,
> our deeper self is designed to serve others.**

Jesus "did not come to be served, but to serve" (Matthew 20:28).
Likewise, our greatest fulfillment comes from serving others—in all
parts of our lives, including our business lives.

It's easier to see how people in certain professions serve others.
Relief workers bring clean water and first aid to victims of natural
disasters. Farmers grow tomatoes and ranchers raise beef to provide
us with the food we need to live. But what about the rest of us?

When I was in the midst of wrestling with the question of
meaning in work, I was an executive at a company that produced
electronic test and measurement equipment. There was nothing
sinister about our products. The company was highly focused on
quality, and to our customers and the people they served, our
equipment was crucial. Without our products, escalators wouldn't
be repaired, data networks wouldn't be installed as efficiently, and
sophisticated test equipment would be out of calibration. But to me,
producing electronic devices hardly seemed to be on a par with

treating cancer. Gradually, though, the connections began to snap into place for me.

By improving our company, I was improving society. People need jobs. I could have a material impact on the number and nature of the jobs we created by contributing to the success of the company. This perspective reinspired me to do my best at what my job asked of me. As a self-starter, I prioritized my activities by the operating maxim to *do what you think is important and do it well.*

And, of course, the implications go well beyond my little world. How do people feel during the hours they are working with us? Are they placed in roles that provide them with an opportunity to express their gifts? Are they inspired by a vision to be a part of something beyond themselves? Do we help them make the connections between their daily work and our higher purpose? I could have a significant influence on the answers to these questions as one of the leaders (servants) of our organization.

Whether it's in the company I work with or in others, I love seeing great service delivered well. It's the welcoming smile of the bellhop at a hotel. It's the empathetic agent at the airline counter saying, "I understand your frustration," as I'm being rebooked after a flight to Europe was delayed and then canceled. It's personal notes, hotel rooms cleaned to perfection, and tasty food served efficiently by a chain of a thousand restaurants because they have thought deeply about the end-to-end service delivery system. It's bank statements redone in a more readable format, clothes cleaned without broken buttons because the cleaner cares, and on and on. Service matters.

The reason I love seeing service delivered with excellence is not really because I like to be pampered. Great service is evidence of a well-run organization. As a fixer, I also see poor service as evidence of a poorly run organization.

And at a deeper level, isn't attention to detail an expression of people doing well what God would have them do well—caring for one another through concrete acts of service?

FOR REFLECTION

■ Reflect on the organization and the job you are currently in. Do any examples come to mind where you have been tempted to be served rather than to serve? How did you respond?

■ In what ways might you serve right where you are? What would it look like to go beyond what's expected, as an act of loving your neighbor? What might be the impediments to performing service at this level? Lack of time? Corporate bureaucracy? Not seeing the opportunities to serve in this way? Personal pride?

36

THE WHY OF BUSINESS

*The LORD God took the man and put him in
the Garden of Eden to work it and take care of it.*

GENESIS 2:15

> ***The purpose of business is to serve—by
> contributing to a better society as seen
> through the eyes of God.***

From the very beginning, humanity has been charged by God with the privilege and the responsibility to take the materials of his creation and make good things out of them. Our work hours certainly aren't the only portion of our lives where this happens, but our jobs are a primary way of cultivating what we have been given.

After years of wrestling, I landed on a functional job definition for myself that has animated my work life for the past twenty-five years: *to contribute to a better society as seen through the eyes of God.*

I believe the fundamental purpose of business is to serve. So if service is at the heart of business, what are the distinctive ways business serves society? Certainly there are many ways, but four have become paramount to me:

1. Responsible Value-Creation. While money is not the comprehensive solution to the world's problems, economic value is a hallmark of a well-functioning society. At a minimum, it is an indication of human flourishing, as people and their talents are set free to contribute without encumbrance or restriction.

As I have reflected on the ways business contributes to society achieving its potential, I am struck by a foundational idea: Business is the only institution that creates economic value. All other institutions distribute it.

This insight brought me into a new level of personal freedom.

I had always been driven to increase the stock price of the companies I helped lead, but I had wondered if it was just to thicken my wallet or whether it might be rooted in a more noble ambition. I could now explain the more complete rationale for taking my first job out of Harvard Business School. The salary at that company was the lowest of the five offers I received, but the equity incentive was the highest. I was energized by the prospect of growing a company and in the process creating significant economic value for its shareholders, including me.

I suppose my motivations will always be mixed this side of heaven, but now I could put my weight down on an explanation that made sense to me (even as a part of me calculates the value of my options in the back room). Paul tells us, "It is fine to be zealous, provided the purpose is good" (Galatians 4:18). If economic value-creation is a God-ordained distinctive of business, I am set free to pursue this purpose with all my zeal.

2. Creating an environment for employees that enables them to grow into the full expression of themselves. Seeing people through the eyes of faith changes everything. Our coworkers are God's creation, made in his image. We have a mandate to treat his people with the "weight of glory" they carry, as C. S. Lewis put it in his book of the same name.

As a senior leader of a business, I significantly affect the lives of my coworkers. During the time I was clarifying these ideas, I multiplied the twenty-five hundred employees at our company by the one hundred thousand hours we'll work in our lifetime (hey, I'm a math guy). That's 250 million hours of work. Will they enjoy their jobs because of me, or are my actions the equivalent of sending them to the dentist's office to have their teeth drilled?

After helping to build or turn around eight businesses, I've concluded that the best way to create a positive environment for employees is to make the business successful. A company built on a financially sustainable business model provides the foundation for creating opportunity for its people. A growing business creates more jobs, provides career paths for employees, and provides opportunities for people to express their skills as they meet the challenges of growth.

Having been involved with hiring thousands of people to keep up with the hypergrowth in building companies *and* having to lay off people to preserve others, I can definitively say the former is way more fun for everybody. We all want to be on a winning team, even if success means saving and re-accelerating companies requiring a dramatic turnaround.

3. Serving customers. This is a particularly tangible way for businesses to contribute to society as seen through the eyes of God.

I purposefully spent many hours in the call center of one internet-based communication services company I served. Sitting in our service center listening to customer-care calls was a wonderful way to experience how we helped people by saving money on their phone bills and connecting them with their families around the world.

We worship a relevant God. He designed us and knows we need food, clothing, and shelter to survive. He also knows that even electronic test tools and communication services delivered with excellence contribute to a flourishing society. Customers are ultimately individuals, each made in the image of God. As we serve our customers, we are serving God.

4. Being a valued corporate citizen. I believe businesses and our people have a responsibility to contribute to the communities where we operate. Our businesses can provide money, people, and an example for others to follow. We can also demonstrate our commitment to environmental stewardship and to transparent and effective corporate governance. I believe businesses also play an important societal role in creating a workforce and working environments that are diverse, inclusive, and collaborative. I'm grateful to have had the opportunity to build strong leadership teams, made stronger by diverse people bringing varying backgrounds and perspectives to our work.

There are so many ways, big and small, to live out our corporate citizenship. At one company where I worked, we spent a Saturday helping build a home for Habitat for Humanity with our coworkers and our families. At another, our executives cooked hamburgers for the emergency relief workers after a hurricane devastated the town in Florida where our company employed hundreds of people in a call center. At a third company, we offered our customers free calling to Japan after a tsunami devastated the country, leaving family members worried and wanting to stay connected.

As our eyes grow more focused on the things of God, we see these distinctives of business not as sideline activities led by the public relations department but as opportunities to be the hands and feet of God in a broken world crying for his love. This stuff matters. The world needs help, and business can do its part as an honorable citizen of the world.

FOR REFLECTION

- Think about the place where you currently work and the goods and services your organization delivers. In what tangible, concrete ways do these outputs contribute to a better society as seen through the eyes of God?

- As you reflect on these four ways business serves society, can you see how your organization contributes along these dimensions? How would you rate your progress in each of them?

37

INVESTING IN OTHERS

We are God's handiwork, created in Christ Jesus
to do good works, which God prepared in advance
for us to do.

EPHESIANS 2:10

There is neither Jew nor Gentile, neither slave nor free,
nor is there male and female, for you are all one in
Christ Jesus.

GALATIANS 3:28

> *People achieving their potential promotes*
> *human flourishing in all its dimensions.*

As I've progressed through my career, I've found myself leading from a deepened center. I can more naturally be who I am and let the work flow from the heart of my being. My judgment has been honed. I'm able to rely on an intuition that has proved its perspicacity through uncountable situations and decisions. As I become less and God becomes more in me, that which flows from me can become more good, more beautiful, and more true. I'm also more keenly aware of my foibles, but I am less angered by them and more likely to simply add them to God's and my to-do list.

There is no place where the convergence between who we are and what we do is more evident than in helping people grow and building effective, well-functioning teams. Surely this is part of the work God prepared in advance for us to do.

As my career has progressed, I have become more and more grateful for the people and the ways we have worked together in low-ego, high-performance teams. One of the great joys of my business life has been playing some small part in helping people grow into more than they even dreamed for themselves.

I saw this in one company where I worked alongside a talented woman who possessed exceptional business judgment, always followed through, and had a strong background in strategy and finance. Her planning skills and business acumen were a primary reason we exceeded our projections to Wall Street many quarters in a row. Though she was hesitant to take on the highest level of executive responsibility, over a couple of years she grew to see her true capability with the support of her colleagues and elevated her sights to include the C-suite as her ultimate career aspiration. On the day her promotion was announced she was flooded with an outpouring of support, and many inside and outside our company have sought her out for her counsel and to hear her story.

Our organizational lives provide an important opportunity for the promotion of people and their talents. And our businesses can benefit enormously from talented people who bring a diversity of perspectives and backgrounds to the table. But we don't have to wait until the end of our careers to help others who still have a big chunk of their career ahead of them.

Once I was asked to write an article, which we called "Mentoring Matters," for our company's internal website. The article was headlined by the observation "It is a great gift to have someone believe in us for who we are that we might grow into who we can become." I've had several people play this role in my life, and as I've progressed through my career, I have had the privilege of serving in this role for many others. I have been honored to be a "holistic accompanist to these folks who have become friends."

During the purposeful pause I took at age fifty, I had a list of twenty-seven younger people who, if they called, I would automatically say yes to having a cup of coffee or lunch with them. I don't call these kinds of relationships "mentoring." I call them "intergenerational friendships" for two reasons. First, being called a mentor implies I have something to say or to give, and that in itself can be intimidating. Second, mentoring implies that it is a one-way relationship, and that is absolutely not the case. While I might be able to help a younger person avoid some of the potholes I have fallen into, I derive great energy from the next generation. I learn from their sense of wonder and their anticipation of having more years ahead of them than behind them.

I believe the greatest compliment that can be paid to a teacher is seeing those they teach become better than their teacher. It has certainly been a great gift to see people succeed beyond my capabilities and their expectations.

As I prepare to retire from a full-time executive role at the time of this writing, I look forward to an "encore calling" that includes investing in the next generation of Christ-following leaders who are called to live fully for God in the world. I know they will leave the world a better place.

FOR REFLECTION

- What are some ways you have been or could be called to help others grow?
- Are you threatened by or energized by seeing others do things better than you could do them yourself?

38

TWO WAYS OF LOOKING AT WEALTH

*Zacchaeus stood up and said to the Lord,
"Look, Lord! Here and now I give half of my
possessions to the poor, and if I have cheated
anybody out of anything, I will pay back
four times the amount."*

*Jesus said to him, "Today salvation has
come to this house, because this man, too,
is a son of Abraham."*

LUKE 19:8-9

> **Viewing wealth as a goal to be achieved
> is burdensome. Seeing it as a gift to be
> shared is freeing.**

Ah, the idol of money. How powerful it is! How attractive! We seem to instinctively order our lives around pursuing it, seeking to grow it and spend it to maximize our own happiness. As much as we say we don't, and wish we didn't, to what degree do we worship money within our hearts?

John D. Rockefeller, one of the richest people ever to have lived, was asked, "How much money is enough?"

"Just a little bit more," he quipped.

That story is still retold today because the motivation behind it is so universal. But Rockefeller was really echoing something the Preacher recognized some three thousand years earlier: "Whoever loves money never has enough" (Ecclesiastes 5:10). When we want more and more, we fail to realize how much power we're allowing money to have over us.

The slave-master relationship between us and money is so easily inverted, like the pull of a magnet inverting the pole of another when it comes into its field. "No one can serve two masters. Either you will hate the one and love the other, or you will be devoted to the one and despise the other. You cannot serve both God and money" (Matthew 6:24).

So how do we live and work in the world of business whose central measure of success is how much money our business is making? How are we to live in this world of wealth dominated by an idol that unceasingly holds out a cup of saltwater with the promise that it will quench our thirst?

In chapter five I told the story of being asked to take charge of the telecommunications company operating in Brazil. What I didn't say was that when I joined as the CFO, I also saw it as my chance to achieve financial independence. I relished the idea of no longer having to work for a paycheck.

Linda and I thought it would make a strong statement to the people I was soliciting to invest in the business if we invested alongside them personally. I also wholeheartedly believed in the prospects of the company. Indeed, the stock price tripled in the first year. Financial independence was nearly within our reach . . . but still beyond our grasp.

Two years later, we would lose over a third of our net worth when the company was sold for dimes on the dollar in the broader telecom industry collapse and the accompanying burst of the dot-com bubble.

At the time we made the investment, I hoped our expected return would free me up to do greater things for God. But in retrospect, I believe that the seeds of my desire for financial independence were sown in "the deceitfulness of wealth" of the third soil in Jesus' parable, which chokes the word, making it unfruitful (Matthew 13:22).

The good news is that through this financial loss, I gained a healthier emotional detachment from money. Financial independence had not moved closer for us—it had moved much further away. The loss was painful, but the freedom would become palpable . . . over time.

This experience forced a fundamental shift in my perspective. It taught me to look at money not through the windshield but in the rearview mirror—seeing money not as a goal to be achieved but as a gift to be shared.

Viewing money as a goal messes me up. It inevitably fuels my desire for more.

Viewing money as a result of productive work, as an asset to be managed and shared, frees me up and releases me from its grip. I then see myself as a steward—not of what is mine, but of what has been entrusted to me by God.

A potential consequence of working in business and doing well at it is that we can end up with a pile of money. If that's the case, we are given the responsibility of managing it on the Lord's behalf. We are expected to be wise and faithful in how we invest it—for ourselves, for our loved ones, and for the needs of others in the world.

A Jesuit friend of ours eulogized his devout brother with these poignant words: "Fixed as he was in the things of eternity, he could sit loosely in the things of time." If we are detached from the shiny things of this world, we can be cheerful givers. Generosity flows out of a detachment from money's captivating allure.

And then, as we commit ourselves to stewarding God's money, an interesting thing begins to happen. God enables us to taste the freedom of his gift described in Ecclesiastes 5:19—"When God gives someone wealth and possessions, and the ability to enjoy them, to accept their lot and be happy in their toil—this is a gift of God."

Notice the two gifts embedded in these words. The first gift of wealth and possessions is considerable, but the second gift of the ability to enjoy them is even more significant . . . and perhaps more rare. I'm coming to see that the way to enjoy our wealth and possessions in a godly way is to see it all as a gift. A gift that comes with a responsibility and a recognition that none of it is ours, all of it is God's, and we are but stewards of the wealth and possessions that come our way.

FOR REFLECTION

- Think about your financial situation. Do you feel a sense of freedom around money, or are you enslaved by it?
- Do you view whatever wealth you might have as yours or as God's? How do you use the wealth and possessions you have been given? What is the right balance for you among sharing, saving, and spending?

39

REMEMBER THE POOR

Blessed are you who are poor,
for yours is the kingdom of God.

LUKE 6:20

All they asked was that we should continue
to remember the poor, the very thing I had
been eager to do all along.

GALATIANS 2:10

> *God asks us to help the poor.*
> *He also uses the poor to help us.*

Returning to our home in Bellevue, Washington, after a Word and Communion service at the church up the street, I was filling a bowl with berries for breakfast. As I looked up from the kitchen sink, I saw a hummingbird going about its work. Its long beak touched the heart of first one flowering bud and then another on the blossoming tree outside. The hummingbird was not only gathering its sustenance from the nectar of the flowers: as it went from flower to flower, it was also pollinating the plants so that they might thrive into the next generation.

So it is with us and those who are in poverty. God provides money through our jobs to meet our needs. And this gift is to be shared with others who need our support.

It has been said, "The poor are not a species." They are individuals. Notice Jesus' words: "Whatever you did for one of the least of these brothers and sisters of mine, you did for me" (Matthew 25:40). If we've either done or not done something for just *one* of the least of these, it will not go unnoticed by Christ, for he is in those who are in poverty among us. Mother Teresa had a profound understanding of this mystical truth as she described her work as caring for Jesus himself in the "distressing disguise" of the poor. Surely a rich life in this world must include remembering those without worldly wealth.

Importantly, poverty resides within us as much as it resides in the world outside of us.

But it is also not up to us to do something for *every* one of these least of his brothers. The one starfish we throw back into the water will be deeply appreciative, even if hundreds more line the shore.

Perhaps by sharing our financial wealth with people struggling financially we can be of assistance, provided our acts are motivated by love. A film about Vincent de Paul—recognized as a saint by the Catholic Church for his service to the poor—offers this poignant perspective: "Charity is a heavy burden to carry. . . . It is not enough to give soup and bread. . . . It is only for your love alone that the poor will forgive you the bread you give to them."

The wealthy have something to offer the poor, but the poor also bring much to the wealthy. Those living in poverty often have wealth far beyond the rich in nonfinancial terms. The economically poor are often rich in relationships, rich in compassion, rich in perseverance, and rich in humility and faith that flows from a daily acceptance of the things they cannot change.

How well Linda and I remember visiting the medical outpost in Youngtown, Peru, built on a garbage dump. As we concluded our visit, we sat on the benches in the medical clinic to pray with a group of thirty local women. The vibrant, Spirit-filled prayers of the women, all praying simultaneously, inspired us deeply. But we were caught off guard when they asked at the conclusion of our prayer, "What can we do for you?"

We thought we'd come to help them, and they were asking how *they* could help *us*? By asking the question, they had already done for us more than they could have imagined, as they inverted our perspective of who has more to learn and who has more to give.

So how might we meet the impoverished in their brokenness? Surely it is not with a sense of superiority or out of self-righteousness. No. We are simply "one beggar telling another beggar where he found bread." We meet others in their brokenness in the same way God meets us in our brokenness—through Christ's brokenness.

At the most sacred meal, shortly before his crucifixion, Jesus told his disciples, "This is My body which is given for you" (Luke 22:19 KJ21). Jesus is in our brokenness, and we are in his. It was *for* our sins and *by* our sins that he was put to death. Our awareness of our own brokenness is the first important step toward living in solidarity with the least of these, in us and in the world.

So we pray that God would give us eyes to see his broken and hurting people, starting with the person in the mirror and extending to those in the offices where we work and to people around the world. May we be generous with those around us and receive from them what they offer, trusting God to bring true riches both to us and to them through the power of his love.

FOR REFLECTION

- Begin by reflecting on the ways that you could be impoverished. Then consider the following questions.
- What forms of poverty do you see adjacent to you and around the world? (As a reminder, this poverty could be among the wealthiest people you know.)

- Who are the poor you might remember, and how might you remember them, not out of self-righteousness but in recognition of our shared poverty?

- How have you learned from (or can you learn from) those in poverty who God has put in your path? Can the financially poor teach you how to be rich in relationships, trust, love, or other ways that matter to God?

40

WORKING FOR ETERNITY

You did not choose me, but I chose you and
appointed you so that you might go and bear
fruit—fruit that will last—and so that whatever
you ask in my name the Father will give you.
This is my command: Love each other.

JOHN 15:16-17

> *Everything done out of love for*
> *God will last forever.*

While we are designed to live fully in the present moment, everything
we do for the love of God will carry into eternity. God infuses our
temporal labor with eternal significance.

Jesus instructs us to work for food "that endures to eternal life"
(John 6:27). Since God is eternal, all that he does has eternal consequences. Everything we do for him, and with him, will also endure
for eternity. Paul reinforced the eternal of the spiritual: "What is seen
is temporary, but what is unseen is eternal" (2 Corinthians 4:18).

My friends Jeff Van Duzer and Tim Dearborn, with whom I've had
countless hours of discussion sorting out my confusion over meaning
in work, have both written eloquently on this subject. In his book
Why Business Matters to God (and What Still Needs to Be Fixed), Jeff
puts the role of business in the context of the grand biblical narrative

of creation, fall, redemption, and restoration. He describes us as being co-creators with God in contributing to a better world. Tim similarly describes the ways business can be sacred in his book *Business as a Holy Calling?* The answer to the question in the title is yes, provided we see our work through the eyes of faith.

Though books have been written on how the best companies are "built to last," the only things that truly last are those of God. This understanding has inspired me to focus on the unseen things that matter most, those things that will survive the fire of divine love.

Paul is explicit about the severe testing of our works that will occur at the end:

> No one can lay any foundation other than the one already laid, which is Jesus Christ. If anyone builds on this foundation using gold, silver, costly stones, wood, hay or straw, their work will be shown for what it is, because the Day will bring it to light. It will be revealed with fire, and the fire will test the quality of each person's work. If what has been built survives, the builder will receive a reward. If it is burned up, the builder will suffer loss but yet will be saved—even though only as one escaping through the flames. (1 Corinthians 3:11-15)

So what of our business lives will survive this fire? As I hope our journey together has revealed, God uses our work to do his work in us. Surely the work God has done in shaping our character will last forever.

I believe we will also carry our relationships with God and his people into eternity.

Jesus defined eternal life for us in a conversation with our Father, which we are privileged to overhear. He said, "Now this is eternal life: that they know you, the only true God, and Jesus Christ, whom you have sent" (John 17:3). To know God, to have an intimate relationship with him, *is* eternal life.

And since whatever we have done for one of the least of these we have done for Jesus, that will surely also have eternal consequences, for Jesus is eternal. Perhaps that conversation with the janitor riding up the elevator will be remembered forever, as might thanking the worker on the production line for her attention to quality, or offering stock options to every person in our company's call center that they might share in the value they created.

Because we are all made in the image of God, it is not just what we have done for the least among us that will be remembered, but every act that the Jesus in us does for the Jesus in others.

I had a good friend who led a business that was built through many acquisitions and was later sold for the astronomical sum of $50 billion. A few years after completing this consummating trans-action, he said to me, "It's interesting. I don't remember the details of any of the many transactions we did. What I remember is the people."

God will remember his people and all that we have done with him and for him. Though we may be called to a "self-naughting" life, the work God does in us and through us will not be for naught.

FOR REFLECTION

- Through the eyes of faith, can you see the parts of what you do that will last into eternity?
- Does this perspective cause you to rethink where you place your priorities and how you spend your time?

CONCLUSION

• • •

In Bible history, forty days is a transformative period. Forty days and forty nights of rain separated the pre-flood world from the post-flood world. After his baptism, and before the start of his public ministry, Jesus fasted for forty days and forty nights. The risen Lord appeared to his followers for forty days, preparing them for life after his ascension.

I hope the forty chapters (and perhaps forty days) you have spent walking through *The Spiritual Art of Business* have been transformative for you. Of course, completing them is not the end of anything. Rather, I hope this can become a beginning, a catalyst for the transformation God seeks to continue to work within you, through you, and in the world.

Business can be a tool for enormous good in the world when placed in the hands of God. People in business are responsible for managing trillions of dollars in investment and for billions of jobs around the world. But the way God works through business is through people who are surrendered to him and committed to serving him and his purposes. Through the eyes of faith, we begin to see every moment charged with God. His will and his Word are embedded in our ordinary circumstances. May we have eyes to see what he is asking us to do, who he is asking us to be, right here, right now.

My encouragement to you is this: *However our Lord has spoken to you through this time, helped you process the past, and perhaps*

*prepared you for the future, follow him now in freedom of spirit
without fear or hesitation.* Let the Master Artist lead you in approaching business, not as a cold exercise in power building or
moneymaking, but as a spiritual art whereby God transforms you
and transforms the world for the better. This may or may not
change *what* you do, but it will change *how* you do it and *why* you
do it. The expressions of your life will be brushstrokes of God's
never-ending creativity.

With that in mind, let's take one last look at the Spiritual Art of
Business cycle. Notice that the tail of the cycle leads back to the head.

Figure 2. The Spiritual Art of Business cycle

Being sent into the world doesn't mean we've climbed off the cycle
and left it behind. There comes a time—probably many times—
when we realize that we are still not all we ought to be. We need to
surrender again to Jesus and be *transformed at a deeper level,* allowing God to change our desires and motivations so we are *ever*

more closely aligned with his purposes, and then *be sent again into the world* with greater clarity about what God wants us to accomplish for him.

This is not a one-and-done proposition. Isaiah beautifully describes this repeating cycle as it occurs in nature and in the course of transforming our nature:

As the rain and the snow
   come down from heaven,
and do not return to it
   without watering the earth
and making it bud and flourish,
   so that it yields seed for the sower and bread for the eater,
so is my word that goes out from my mouth:
   It will not return to me empty,
but will accomplish what I desire
   and achieve the purpose for which I sent it.
      (Isaiah 55:10-11)

In the same way that Jesus as the Word made flesh came down from heaven to make us flourish and then returned to heaven, so God's Word is active and transforms us into his likeness. As this repeating pattern takes hold in our lives, our work lives will come alive in Christ so that God might bring life to the world through us and through the work he's given us to do.

This is why I encourage you to hold on to this book. You may want to refer to it again—if not to reread it entirely—at least to revisit certain areas of your life where God is still accomplishing his purposes.

Even more importantly, if you've been using a journal to record the insights from your contemplation, I encourage you to cherish those pages so you can refer to them later. My journals, now totaling over ten thousand pages, are lined in a three-foot row at the bottom of the bookshelf in my office closet. They represent a rich history of my journey with God. May your reflections become as meaningful to you as mine are to me. They are a touchstone to help us remember the great things God has done and continues to do for us.

God uses our work to do his work in us. And as we are transformed by him, he will transform the world through us.

ACKNOWLEDGMENTS

• • •

So many people, circumstances, and experiences have conspired with God to shape this impure lump of clay. Regretfully, I can cite only a few.

First, my parents. You dropped us off a great distance from the womb and were always our greatest cheerleaders. To my five brothers and sisters. What a gift when family become friends. You are among my closest. And even our in-laws. Thank you for being such ardent supporters and faithful pray-ers.

Our dear friends of forty years, the Everitts and Kasts, who invited us to the Colorado camp that would create a defining moment in my spiritual journey. Thank you for introducing us to Jesus and for meeting with this project throughout the following months (and years) of confusion. You were always there to have a beer on a moment's notice, to listen to my questions, and endure my "confusion over Christianity."

For the many men of the men's groups who met in the many cities we lived in across the country and across three decades of walking together. I have been shaped by your challenges and your grace. In particular to Jack McMillan for his model of living an authentic faith in the executive suite. Thank you for responding to my long letter inviting you to be a spiritual mentor when neither of us knew what that meant. And to Connie Jacobsen for putting those groups together that would inspire and challenge us all.

For Tim Dearborn and Jeff Van Duzer. You were patient and faithful friends as I wrestled through the confusion to find meaning in work. For Katherine Leary Alsdorf for being a pioneer in integrating faith and work and for your prayer that landed me almost on target. Now we've all written books birthed out of the journey. For the uncountable other friends who have shaped these ideas, listened to my ramblings, and still asked to continue the conversation, I am immeasurably grateful.

For the coworkers who endured the challenges of business with me. Thank you for your patience in accepting my leadership when it wasn't what any of us wanted it to be.

I thank Jeff Barneson and the many students from the Harvard Business School Christian Fellowship, Mark Washington, and MBA students from around the country for your invitations, our travels, and for advancing these ideas. And to the Adventure with God group—you were among the early guinea pigs . . . though we did pamper you along the way.

I have a long list of folks to credit from InterVarsity, beginning with Bob Fryling, followed by Jeff Crosby, Andy LePeau, Alec Hill, Tom Lin, and now the highly capable Cindy Bunch and, of course, Tianna Haas, who have served as editors for this work. Thank you for your encouragement to distill disparate, extraneous thoughts into something that might be useful to others.

To Eric Stanford who transported my soul in a box—those ten thousand pages of journals—from the trunk of my car to his, wondering what we could do with it all. And to Cliff Johnson who helped sort through which to do first. You were among my first editors and unwavering advocates. Thank you both for supplementing my shallow knowledge of the world of publishing with your deep experience.

Thank you to the dozen beta readers who took your job so seriously, providing comprehensive, personalized feedback on the earliest manuscript. I'd hinged the decision on whether to proceed on

Acknowledgments

the single question of whether this could be helpful to others. Your vulnerable, open responses were the fleece I needed to bring this work from the recesses of my heart into the light of the world.

And, of course, my deepest gratitude to Linda, and Mark and David, to whom this work is dedicated. And to their wives, Elizabeth and Krissy, and now our young grands, for whom we do these things. Thanks be to God for our shared faith in the One who provides us with meaningful work made all the more meaningful through our life-giving relationships.

As a final expression of gratitude, all of the author's net proceeds will go to charitable endeavors focused on enabling people to live fully for God in the world. Thank you for joining us in this great adventure.

ABOUT THE AUTHOR

From a range of C-suite roles, Barry Rowan has been instrumental in building and transforming eight businesses, primarily in the technology and communications space. Barry earned his MBA from Harvard Business School in 1983 and his BS in business administration and chemical biology from the College of Idaho, where he graduated summa cum laude in 1979.

Motivated by his desire to give back, Barry has served as a trustee for two universities, on the board for the entrepreneurial leadership program at another, and as president of a K–12 Christian school. He has also served on the board of InterVarsity, the Harvard Business School Christian Fellowship and Alumni Association, and the National Leadership Council for World Vision.

Having recently retired from a full-time corporate role, Barry is now pursuing an "encore calling," which includes continuing to invest in organizations, impoverished communities, and the next generation of leaders through writing, teaching, consulting, and holistic accompaniment.

One of Barry's great joys is serving alongside Linda, his partner for life. They have two married sons and three beloved grands.

To contact Barry, please go to www.barrylrowan.com, where you can also find a discussion guide for small groups and a media kit for speaking invitations.